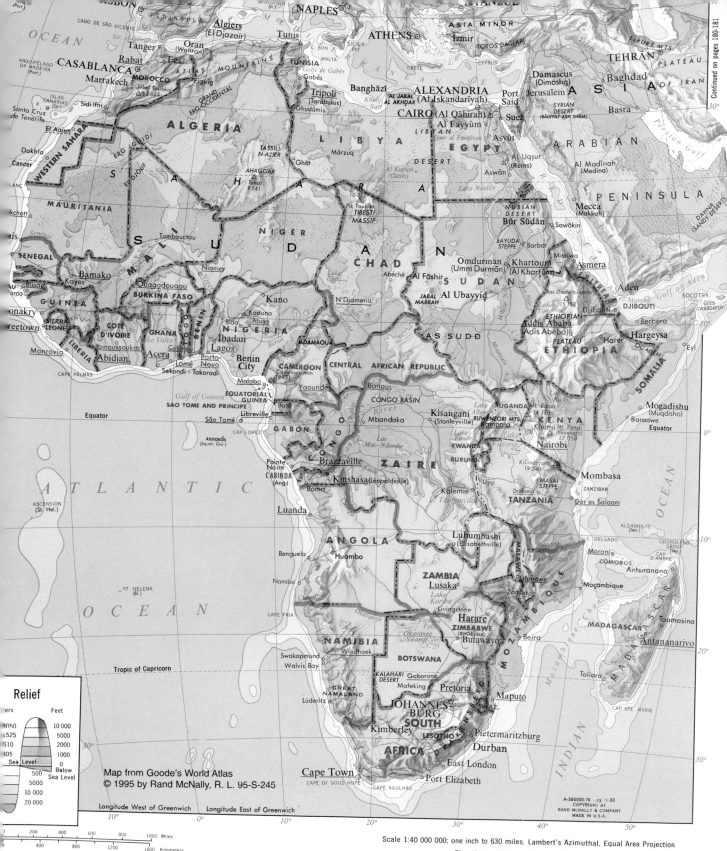

OCEAN

CABO DE SÃO VICENTE

NAPLES

ATHENS

ASIA MINOR

Izmir

TOROS DAGLARI

ELBURZ MTS.

TEHRAN

PLATEAU

Algiers
(El Djazaïr)

Tunis

Damascus
(Dimashq)

Baghdad

OF IRAN

CASABLANCA

Tanger
Oran
(Wahran)

TUNISIA

Jerusalem

A S I A

Basra

Rabat

Fès

SICILY

MALTA

CAP BON

CRETE

CYPRUS

SYRIAN
DESERT
(BĀDIYAT ASH SHĀM)

Marrakech

MOROCCO

ATLAS
MOUNTAINS

Tripoli
(Tarabulus)

Banghāzī

ALEXANDRIA
(Al Iskandarīyah)

Port
Said

Suez

Jebel Toubkal
4 165

Figuig

Golfe de Gabès

Gabès

AL JABAL
AL AKHDAR

CAIRO (Al Qāhirah)

ARABIAN

Sidi Ifni

GRAND
ERG
OCCIDENTAL

Ghudāmis

Al Fayyūm

ISLAS
CANARIAS
(Sp.)

A L G E R I A

L I B Y A

Asyūt

PENINSULA

Santa Cruz
de Tenerife

Mārzuq

EGYPT

Al Uqsur
(Ruins)

Al Madīnah
(Medina)

Cancer

WESTERN
SAHARA

El Aaiún

TASSILI
N'AJJER

Ghāt

DESERT

LIBYAN

Aswān

Mecca
(Makkah)

Dakhla

AHAGGAR

Tahat
9 541

Pic Toussîde

TIBESTI
MASSIF

Aswān

Lake Nasser

NUBIAN
DESERT

DAHNA
(SANDY DESERT)

MAURITANIA

S
A
H
A
R
A

BŪR SŪDĀN

Sawākin

SENEGAL

Tombouctou

M
A
L
I

NIGER

CHAD

BAYUDA
STEPPE

Barbar

Bamako

Niamey

Kano

Abéché

Al Fāshir

Omdurman
(Umm Durmān)

Khartoum
(Al Khartūm)

Mitsiwa

Asmera

Kayes

OUAGADOUGOU

BURKINA FASO

N'Djamena

SUDAN

Ras Dashen Terara
15 158

ERITREA

Aden

GUINEA

Bissau

Kaduna

Abuja

AL Ubayyid

JABAL
MARRAH

Addis Ababa
Adis Abeba

ETHIOPIAN

Djibouti

DJIBOUTI

Berbera

SIERRA
LEONE

Freetown

CÔTE
D'IVOIRE

GHANA

Bida

NIGERIA

Benue

CAMEROON

AS SUDD

PLATEAU

ETHIOPIA

Harer

Hargeysa

Monrovia

LIBERIA

Yamoussoukro

Accra

Lomé

Porto-
Novo

Ibadan

Lagos

Benin
City

Cameroon Mtn.
13 451

Mt. Elgon
14 178

Mt. Kenya
17 058

OGADEN

SOMALIA

Eyl

Abidjan

Sekondi-Takoradi

CENTRAL AFRICAN REPUBLIC

ADAMAOUA

Yaoundé

Bangui

Uele

UGANDA

RUWENZORI MTS.

Kampala

KENYA

Equator

São Tomé

EQUATORIAL
GUINEA

Malabo

Bata

Libreville

GABON

CONGO BASIN

Mbandaka

Kisangani
(Stanleyville)

Lake
Albert

Kisumu
(Kinoyga)

Nairobi

Mogadishu
(Muqdisho)

Baraawe

Equator

SÃO TOMÉ AND PRINCIPE

CAP LOPEZ

CONGO RIVER

RWANDA

BURUNDI

Lake
Edward

Lake
Victoria

Kilimanjaro
19 340

Mombasa

Pointe
Noire

Brazzaville

ZAIRE

Ujiji

Dodoma

MASAI
STEPPE

ZANZIBAR

CABINDA
(Ang.)

Kinshasa (Léopoldville)

Kalemie

TANZANIA

Dar es Salaam

Boma

Lake
Tanganyika

ASCENSION
(St. Hel.)

Luanda

ALDABRA IS.
(Sey.)

CAP DELGADO

COSMOLEDO
GROUP

Lubumbashi
(Elisabethville)

Moroni

CAP
D'AMBRE

Antsiranana

ATLANTIC

ANGOLA

COMOROS

Benguela

Huambo

Lake
Nyasa

Moçambique

MADAGASCAR

ST HELENA
(Br.)

Namibe

ZAMBIA

MALAWI

Lilongwe

Lusaka

Zomba

Harare

OCEAN

CAPE FRIA

Okavango

Victoria
Falls

Lake
Kariba

Livingstone

MOZAMBIQUE

ZIMBABWE
(RHODESIA)

Bulawayo

Beira

Taamasina

Antananarivo

Tropic of Capricorn

Swakopmund

Walvis Bay

NAMIBIA

Windhoek

KALAHARI
DESERT

Gaborone

BOTSWANA

Okavango
Swamp

Pretoria

Maputo

Toliara

CAP STE. MARIE

INDIAN

Lüderitz

GREAT
NAMALAND

Mafeking

JOHANNES-
BURG

SWAZ.

OCEAN

Kimberley

SOUTH

LESOTHO

Pietermaritzburg

AFRICA

Cape Town

CAPE OF GOOD HOPE

East London

Durban

Port Elizabeth

CAPE AGULHAS

A-580000-76   -13 16-33
COPYRIGHT BY
RAND McNALLY & COMPANY
MADE IN U.S.A.

Relief

Meters   Feet

3050   10 000
1525   5000
610   2000
305   1000
Sea Level   Sea Level
              0
500   Below
5000   Sea Level
10 000
20 000

Longitude West of Greenwich   Longitude East of Greenwich
            10°   0°   10°

200   400   600   800   1000 Miles
   400   800   1200   1600 Kilometers

Scale 1:40 000 000; one inch to 630 miles. Lambert's Azimuthal, Equal Area Projection
Elevations and depressions are given in feet.

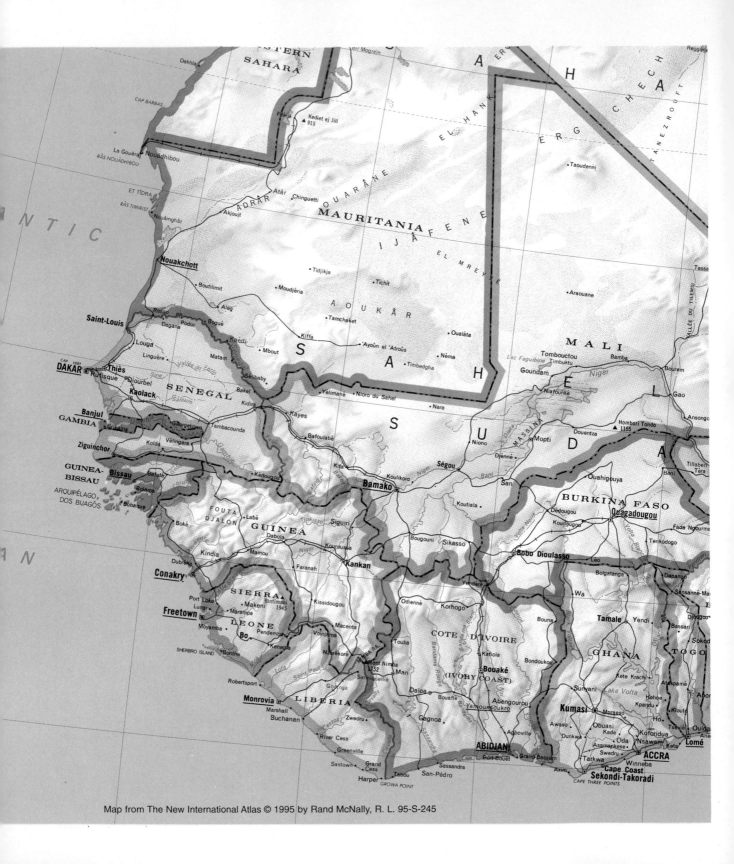

WESTERN
SAHARA
Dakhla
Cap BARBAS
CAP BARBAS
La Gouéra•Nouâdhibou
RÂS NOUÂDHIBOU
ET TÎDRA
RÂS TIMIRIST

Aïr Mogrein
Fdérik   ▲Kediet ej Jill
915

A   ERG   H   CHECH   A
TANEZROUFT
Reggane

Taoudenni

OUARÂNE   EL   HANK   ERG

ADRAR   Atâr• Chinguetti
Akjoujt
Nouâmghâr

MAURITANIA   F   E   N   E

IJÂ
EL MREYYE

Nouakchott
•Boutilimit
•Tidjikja
•Moudjéria
•Tichît
A   O   U   K   Â   R
EL MREYYE

Tessal

Araouane

Saint-Louis   Rosso   Aleg   •Bogué   Kiffa
Dagana   Podor
Louga   Kaédi
CAP   VERT   Linguère   Matam
DAKAR   Thiès   Diourbel   Sélibaby
Rufisque   SENEGAL   Kidira
Kaolack   Saloum   Bakel
Banjul   Tambacounda   Kayes
GAMBIA   Brikama   Georgetown
Ziguinchor   Kolda   Bafoulabé
Vélingara   Kédougou   Kita
GUINEA-   Bafatá   Koulikoro
BISSAU   Bissau   Siguiri   Bamako
Boke   Bolama   Labé   Ségou
ARQUIPÉLAGO   Bubaque   FOUTA   Dabola   Bougouni   Sikasso
DOS BIJAGÓS   DJALON   GUINEA
Kindia   Mamou   Faranah   Kankan
Dubréka   Kourous sa
Conakry   Kissidougou

Tamchaket
Kiffa   •'Ayoûn el 'Atroûs   •Néma
Yélimané   Nioro du Sahel   Nara
Timbedgha

Tombouctou   Bamba
Timbuktu   Bourem
Lac Faguibine
Goundam   Niger   Gao
Niafounké   E
L   Ansongo
MASSINA   Douentza   ▲Hombori Tondo   Tillaberi
Mopti   1155   Téra
Niono   D   U   A
Djenné   Ouahigouya   Bani
San   Ouagadougou
Koutiala   BURKINA FASO
Dédougou   Ouagadougou
Koudougou   Fada Ngourma
Bobo Dioulasso   Tenkodogo
Léo   Bolgatanga   Dapango
Yendére   Wa   Sansanné-Ma

SIERRA
Makeni   Bintimani   Kissidougou
Lungi   1945
Freetown   Marampa
LEONE   Pendembu   Kenema
Bo
SHERBRO ISLAND   Bonthe
Moyamba   Nzérékoré
Lofa   Voinjama   Macenta
Robertsport   Ghanga
Monrovia   LIBERIA
Marshall   Zwedru
Buchanan
River Cess
Greenville
Sastown   Grand
Cess
Harper   GROWA POINT

Odienné   Korhogo
Touba   Bouna
Man   Katiola
Mont Nimba   COTE D'IVOIRE
1752   Bouaké
Samniquellie   (IVORY COAST)
Daloa   Bouafle
Gagnoa   Yamoussoukro
Abengourou
Agboville
Sassandra   ABIDJAN
San-Pédro   Port-Bouët   Grand-Bassam
Tabou   Axim   CAPE THREE POINTS

Tamale   Yendi
Bassari
Bondoukou   GHANA   Sokode
Sunyani   Kete Krachi   TOGO
Lake Volta   Hohoe
Kpandu
Kumasi   Mpraeso   Ho
Awaso   Kpalimé
Obuasi   Kade   Koforidua
Dunkwa   Oda   Nsawam   Keta   Lomé
Asamankese   Swedru
Tarkwa   Winneba
ACCRA
Cape Coast
Sekondi-Takoradi

Enchantment of the World

CÔTE D'IVOIRE
(IVORY COAST)

by Patricia K. Kummer

Consultant for Côte d'Ivoire: Robert G. Launay, Ph.D., Professor of Anthropology, Northwestern University, Evanston, Illinois

CHILDREN'S PRESS®
A Division of Grolier Publishing
New York • London • Hong Kong • Sydney
Danbury, Connecticut

Boys and young men in a fishing village along the southern coast

Project Editor: Mary Reidy
Design: Jean Blashfield Black
Photo Research: Feldman & Associates, Inc.

Library of Congress Cataloging-in-Publication Data

Kummer, Patricia K.
    Côte d'Ivoire (Ivory Coast) / Patricia K. Kummer.
       p. cm. -- (Enchantment of the world)
    Includes index.
    Summary: Describes the geography, history, culture, economy, people, and cities of the West African country of Côte d'Ivoire.
    ISBN 0-516-02641-0
    1. Côte d'Ivoire--Juvenile literature. [1. Côte d'Ivoire.] I. Title. II. Series.
DT545.22.K86 1996
966.68--dc20
                                      95-33594
                                         CIP
                                         AC

Picture Acknowledgments:
AP/Wide World Photos: 46, 63 (left), 88, 89, 105
Archive Photos-France: 47
The Bettmann Archive: 37
Bettmann Newsphotos: 42, 43, 45, 49 (left), 53

© **Pat Roddy/Boltin Picture Library:** 26 (2 photos), 34, 61 (left), 73, 87, 91 (right), 95, 109 (left)
H. Armstrong Roberts: 21 (left); © **Len Rue, Jr.,** 6; © **Camerique,** 10 (top); © **J. Patton,** 20 (right); © **Blumebild,** 24
© **Dave G. Houser:** 32, 82 (left), 97, 103
Impact Visuals: © **Hollandse Hoogt Jan,** 50, 52, 56
North Wind Picture Archives: 30, 31
Odyssey/Frerck/Chicago: © **Robert Frerck,** 71
Photri: 5 (left), 17, 18 (top and bottom left), 21 (bottom right), 23 (bottom right), 39 (left), 55, 70 (right), 74, 80 (right), 91 (left), 100 (left), 106 (left), 109 (right); © **D. Forbert,** 4, 18 (bottom left), 20 (left), 68 (bottom and top left)
Reuters/Bettmann: 59
Root Resources: © **Lois Coren,** 69 (left), 101 (left)
SuperStock International, Inc.: Cover, 78 (left), 85, 93 (bottom and top right), 98, 102, 106 (right); © **Emanuel Nado,** 5 (right); © **David Forbert,** 9, 41; © **Michele Burgess,** 10 (bottom), 112; © **The Photo Source,** 15, 83, 90 (left); © **Hubertus Kanus,** 36, 66 (right); © **Hoa-Qui,** 39 (right), 49 (right), 68 (top right), 86, 101 (right); © **Kurt Scholz,** 64; © **World Photo Service Ltd.,** 70 (left), 75; © **Age Fotostock,** 76
Tony Stone Images: © **Christoph Burki,** 12, 78 (top and bottom right), 93 (left), 107; © **Julian Calder,** 68 (bottom right)
Tropix: © **M & V Birley,** 61 (right), 63 (right), 66 (left), 77, 80 (left), 96
Valan: © **James D. Markou,** 13, 22 (top); © **Val & Alan Wilkinson,** 18 (bottom right); © **Tom Parkin,** 18 (top right); © **Stephen J. Krasemann,** 21 (top right); © **Jean Sloman,** 22 (bottom); © **Christine Osborne,** 23 (left), 69 (right); © **Aubrey Lang,** 23 (top right); © **Karl Weidmann,** 33
© **Brian Vikander:** 28, 82 (right), 90 (right), 100 (right), 108, 110 (2 photos), 111

Cover: A village about 60 miles (97 kilometers) from Abidjan

Two women of Ivory Coast — modern and traditional

TABLE OF CONTENTS

Chapter 1   *The Jewel of West Africa* (Introduction) 7

Chapter 2   *A Varied Landscape* (Geography) 11

Chapter 3   *Native Kingdoms and European Explorers* (Prehistory to the 1800s) 25

Chapter 4   *From French Colony to Independent Nation* (1893 to the Present) 35

Chapter 5   *Stability, Progress, and Compromise* (Government, Education, and Health) 54

Chapter 6   *Rebuilding the Ivorian Miracle* (Economy, Transportation, and Communication) 65

Chapter 7   *The People and Culture of Côte d'Ivoire* (Ethnic Groups, Religion, the Arts, and Festivals) 79

Chapter 8   *A Tour Through Côte d'Ivoire* (Cities and Villages) 99

Mini-Facts at a Glance 113

Index 124

Elephants, for which Ivory Coast is named, are still found in the country,
though in dwindling numbers. This one is sharing water with a marabou stork.

Chapter 1

THE JEWEL OF
WEST AFRICA

Since receiving its independence in 1960, Ivory Coast has served as a model of economic prosperity and political stability for other West African countries. Ivory Coast's closest West African neighbors are Liberia and Guinea to the west, Mali and Burkina Faso to the north, and Ghana to the east. The Gulf of Guinea, an arm of the Atlantic Ocean, splashes to the south.

On a map, Ivory Coast looks like a raggedly cut square. Its 124,503 square miles (322,463 square kilometers) make it a little larger than New Mexico. Most of this West African country lies on a large plateau. Coastal lagoons, rain forests, a broad savanna or grassland, and rugged highlands provide Ivory Coast with a varied landscape.

More than five hundred years ago, Portuguese traders gave Ivory Coast its name. In the late 1400s they sailed around the bulge of West Africa looking for a route to Asia. Along the way the Portuguese found West African people willing to trade ivory elephant tusks. Today, an elephant head surrounded by palm trees is the symbol of Ivory Coast.

Ivory Coast first attracted French interest in the 1600s. During brief periods from that time until the 1880s, French missionaries and traders exercised varying degrees of influence in coastal areas. Beginning in 1886 the French government made a concerted effort to bring all of Ivory Coast under its control. From 1916 to 1960 all of present-day Ivory Coast was a French colony. Today French influence still remains visible in Ivory Coast. The official name of Ivory Coast is *République de Côte d'Ivoire*. That's French for Republic of Ivory Coast. The Ivorian people call their country *Côte d'Ivoire* for short. French is Ivory Coast's official language. Many French people still hold advisory positions in the government and own or manage Ivorian companies.

Many present-day Ivorians belong to ethnic groups that lived in Ivory Coast before the Portuguese traders arrived. They continue the traditions of their ancestors. In this way, Ivorian culture presents a rich mosaic of languages, religions, arts, and crafts.

Félix Houphouët-Boigny represented the blending of Ivorian and French cultures. A French-trained medical doctor, Houphouët-Boigny belonged to Ivory Coast's largest ethnic group—the Baule people. Houphouët-Boigny led the Ivory Coast to independence but maintained close ties with France. In his old age, Ivorians respectfully called him *Le Vieux*, "The Old Man." Until his death in 1993, Houphouët-Boigny served as Ivory Coast's president. He guided the country's economy by encouraging trade with France and by developing Ivory Coast's agriculture. When Henri Konan Bédié, the leader of Ivory Coast's legislature, peacefully succeeded Houphouët-Boigny as president, Ivorians and the rest of the world hoped that Ivory Coast would continue its role as the "Jewel of West Africa."

Only a few miles along the coast from the huge, thriving city of Abidjan, people in lagoon fishing villages live as they always have.

Above: The grassland, or savanna, of Ivory Coast is home to many of the most famous mammals in the world, including African lions. Their numbers are now few.
Below: The major city, Abidjan, is located on one of the many lagoons along the coast.

Chapter 2

A VARIED LANDSCAPE

Ivory Coast lies between five and ten degrees north of the equator. Most of Ivory Coast is a large plateau, tilting gradually south toward the Gulf of Guinea. On this plateau are the lagoon region in the southeast, the rain forest in the southwest and east-central, and the savanna region in the north. In the northwest, mountain peaks rise to more than 6,000 feet (1,829 meters) in the Nimba Mountains of the Guinea Highlands. Each of these regions has its own distinctive plant and animal life.

THE LAGOON REGION

The wide lagoon region extends west about 200 miles (322 kilometers) along the Gulf of Guinea from the border with Ghana. Over the centuries, crashing surf and strong ocean currents have built up a strip of sandbars, or barrier islands. Some sandbars are as much as 4 miles (6.4 kilometers) wide with smooth beaches. For centuries, the sandbars kept large ships from landing at Ivory Coast.

Between the sandbars and the coastline are narrow lagoons. The Tadio, Ébrié, and Aby Lagoons are connected to one another by a network of canals. Coastal cities such as Assini, Grand-Bassam, and Grand-Lahou have developed in the lagoon region.

A pool located within the tangled rain forest

Abidjan, Ivory Coast's largest city and first deep-water port, is also located in the region. Inland from the lagoons, the land is flat and is used for farms and plantations.

THE RAIN FOREST REGION

Ivory Coast's rain forest lies north and west of the lagoon region. Covering one-third of the country, this region extends from Ghana to Liberia. West of the Sassandra River, the thick equatorial forest stretches to the Gulf of Guinea. Ivory Coast's western coast, much rougher than the lagoon region in the east, is broken up by

The powerful and fast-moving African buffalo grazes on water plants, forest leaves, and savanna grasses.

small cliffs and rocky points. The deep-water port at San Pédro now makes shipping possible from the west coast.

Inland, small hills accent the ground's otherwise gentle roll throughout the entire region. Near the western city of Man are the Nimba Mountains. Mount Nimba, on the Liberia-Guinea-Ivory Coast border, is Ivory Coast's highest peak at 5,748 feet (1,752 meters). Yamoussoukro, Ivory Coast's new capital, stands in the middle of the rain forest's northern edge.

THE SAVANNA REGION

The northern two-thirds of the country is covered by savanna. As a traveler moves north from the rain forest, trees gradually become smaller and grow alone or in small clumps. There also are fewer varieties. Sandy soil and short grasses are other features of the savanna's gently rolling plain. The wide-open spaces and drought-resistant grasses of the savanna provide grazing for Ivory Coast's few cattle. The region's soil lends itself to growing cotton —the savanna's largest cash crop.

From the city of Korhogo to Odienné in the northwest corner, the savanna rises up into the Guinea Highlands. Mount Tonkou, at 4,260 feet (1,298 meters), is the region's highest peak. Small groups of hills dot the land between the city of Ferkéssédougou and the border with Ghana to the east. In the far northeastern section of the savanna, 4,500 square miles (11,655 square kilometers) make up Komoé National Park. Bouaké, the country's second-largest city, thrives on the southern stretches of the savanna.

RIVERS AND LAKES

Four major rivers—the Cavally, Sassandra, Bandama, and Komoé—run north to south through Ivory Coast. They empty into the Gulf of Guinea. Because of rapids and waterfalls, only 30 to 50 miles (48 to 80 kilometers) of each river are navigable. Even those few miles become unnavigable when the rivers flood during the rainy seasons and dry up during the dry seasons. The importance of the country's rivers is their potential for producing hydro-electric power.

The Cavally, westernmost of the rivers, begins in the Nimba Mountains and forms most of Ivory Coast's border with Liberia. Its mouth at the Gulf of Guinea is narrow and blocked by dangerous rocks and sandbars.

Just east of Odienné, the Sassandra River begins its 350-mile (563-kilometer) course to the gulf. Its main tributaries are the Nzo and Lobo Rivers. Since 1982 dams providing hydroelectric power for the western part of the country have been built. One is located where the Nzo joins the Sassandra at Buyo. The second dam is to the south at Soubré. Large lakes formed behind these dams. The port city of Sassandra stands at the river's mouth.

Mount Tonkou, the highest point in northern Ivory Coast

The 500-mile (805-kilometer)-long Bandama River winds its way down the center of the country, emptying into Tadio Lagoon across from Grand-Lahou. It eventually reaches the gulf by passing between barrier islands. From its many tributaries, including the Red Bandama, the White Bandama, and the Nzi Rivers, the Bandama drains more than half the land of Ivory Coast. In 1972 a dam and hydroelectric plant were completed on the river just north of Yamoussoukro, doubling Ivory Coast's production of electricity. The 650-square-mile (1,684-square-kilometer) Kossou Lake was created north of the dam. During the 1980s, another dam was built farther south on the Bandama. Taabo Lake formed behind that dam.

From its source in Burkina Faso, the Komoé River flows through eastern Ivory Coast before it spills into the Ébrié Lagoon near Grand-Bassam. Like the Bandama, the Komoé reaches the gulf by winding through barrier islands. The Komoé's main tributaries are the Leraba, Iringo, and Kongo Rivers.

In the country's southeast corner, the Bia River flows from Ghana to the Aby Lagoon. The Bia provides a trade route for farm products from the city of Aboisso to the coast. North of Aboisso, in 1959, Ivory Coast's first dam and hydroelectric plant were completed on the Bia. In 1964 a second dam was built.

CLIMATE AND SEASONS

Situated just north of the equator, Ivory Coast's climate is marked by year-round high temperatures. Large amounts of rain fall during specific months of the year. Because of these conditions, the country's seasons are divided into rainy and dry rather than winter, spring, summer, and fall.

Each year coastal and rain forest regions experience two rainy seasons, from May to July and October through November, and two dry seasons, from December to May and July to October. On the drier, northern savanna, there is one long rainy season from May to November and one long dry season from November to May. In the mountains of the savanna, there is no dry season.

A high of 120 degrees Fahrenheit (49 degrees Celsius) was recorded on the savanna at Ferkéssédougou. In addition to the

The high humidity and frequent rain of a tropical region supports the tall trees and thick undergrowth typical of a rain forest. The harmattan wind from the Sahara has no effect on the rain forest.

high temperatures, people on the savanna must contend with the yearly *harmattan*, a cold, dry northeasterly wind that blows down from the Sahara desert during the early months of the dry season. Although the drying effect of the harmattan wind reaches the coastal region, it lasts for only short periods in December and January. With average humidity readings of 70 to 80 percent, the climate of the coastal region is like that of Washington, D.C., in the summer.

Important trees of Ivory Coast include (clockwise from top left): the baobab; breadfruit, which is used for eating; the oil palm, which has brightly colored fruits that produce oil used for cooking; and the economically important rubber tree, which is seen here being tapped for its useful sap.

PLANT LIFE

Large stands of native oil palm and coconut trees flourish on the edges of the lagoons and the coast. Banana, cocoa, and coffee trees have been introduced in the region for their commercial value.

In parts of the forest untouched by humans, broad-leaved evergreens form thick canopies that cover the ground at heights of 70 to 80 feet (21 to 24 meters). Oil palm, banana, cocoa, and coffee trees also flourish amid the remains of the rain forest. At one time, Ivory Coast's rain forest was one of the largest on the African continent. In 1960 rain forest covered 40 million acres (16 million hectares). By the 1980s it had dwindled to about 13.6 million acres (5.5 million hectares). Excessive cutting by the timber industry and the clearing of land to plant cash crops and to build roads were the main reasons for this decline. To save the rain forest, the government of Ivory Coast has set aside 8.6 million acres (3.5 million hectares) as a permanent forest reserve. The government also has reduced the number of trees that can be cut each year and now requires that 24,691 acres (10,000 hectares) be reforested annually.

The dense rain forest contains valuable hardwood trees used for making furniture, cabinets, and decorative objects. Chief among these trees are mahogany, iroko (African teak), sipo, niangon, and avodire trees. Samba is an important softwood. Other trees of the rain forest include various kinds of rubber trees.

In the southwest forest, the United Nations Educational, Scientific, and Cultural Organization (UNESCO) has set aside Tai National Park as part of the world's heritage. It includes the only primary rain forest left in Africa. Air plants such as orchids and

Rain forests produce hardwood for export (left) and are home to dangerous snakes, such as the rhinoceros viper (right).

mosses flourish amid the trees of the rain forest where the plants can grow without their roots in soil. Lianas, or woody vines, wind themselves around tree trunks or hang from high branches. Ferns carpet the forest floor.

In the dry heat of the savanna, the few stands of trees grow mainly along the riverbanks. Their deep roots seek out underground moisture during the dry season. Sau trees grow from 30 to 60 feet (9 to 18 meters) high and are used for lumber. Sheabutter, dry-zone mahogany, baobab, and acacia trees stand out on the grasslands. The breadfruit tree, whose fruit looks like bread when it is baked, also grows on the savanna.

ANIMAL LIFE

Ivory Coast's government has taken steps to protect the country's wildlife by setting aside land for national parks and

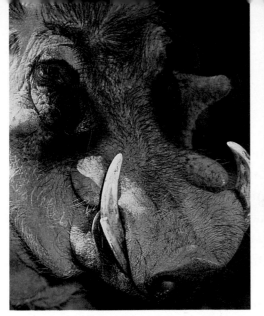

Some mammals of the Ivory Coast include (clockwise from top left): a warthog, close up; a family of waterbucks; and two hippopotamuses confronting each other.

wildlife reserves. Tai National Park provides a home for pygmy hippopotamuses, chimpanzees, and several kinds of antelopes. Anthropologists who studied chimpanzees in Tai National Park discovered that chimpanzees hunt together and then share the food. They use tools, such as rocks or sticks, to open nuts. The Mount Nimba Reserve, shared by Ivory Coast, Liberia, and Guinea, protects forest buffaloes, reddish-brown antelopes, yellow-backed antelopes, bushbucks, chevrotains, and tree hyraxes. Visitors are not allowed in the reserve.

Komoé National Park in Ivory Coast's northeastern corner is the country's largest national park or animal reserve. Buffaloes, hippopotamuses, elephants, and lions are supposed to be able to

roam freely. In 1974 the government passed a law against shooting any of the park's wild animals, but Lobi hunters, among others, do not honor this law. The Lobi have also set up small villages at the park's north end where they plant yams and millet.

Elephants, whose tusks gave Ivory Coast its name, are rare today because of the lucrative ivory trade. By limiting hunting to protect the remaining herds, the government hopes to increase the elephant population. But poachers, who illegally kill elephants, continue to threaten the herds.

Antelope, black buffaloes, gazelles, kob antelopes, lions, and water bucks range over the grassy savanna. A variety of small monkeys, small red buffaloes, wild hogs, and red river hogs live in the southern rain forest. Crocodiles and hippopotamuses enjoy lying in the southern rivers. Birds in the region include bush fowl, quail, and partridges. Green and yellow bulbuls and noisy black-and-white hornbills nest in the rain forest's trees. Lagoon birds include ducks, egrets, herons, plovers, and terns. Barracuda, carp, cavally, mackerel,

Two primates found in the forests of Ivory Coast are an endangered chimpanzee (top) and a rare black-and-white colobus monkey (bottom).

A huge termite mound beside an acacia tree (above);
a red-billed hornbill of forested areas (top right);
and a reef heron of coastal waters (right)

marlin, mullet, sardines, shark, tarpon, and tuna swim in the lagoons and the Gulf of Guinea. Cobras, green mambas, and pythons are a few of the dangerous snakes that slither through Ivory Coast.

Ivory Coast's hot, humid climate breeds a large variety of insects, including some species that are deadly to humans. The tsetse fly, which carries sleeping sickness, breeds in Ivory Coast. This disease can cause victims to lapse into a coma and even die. The anopheles mosquito carries malaria, which brings on chills and fever. Other mosquitoes transmit yellow fever and dengue fever. Yellow fever is marked by weakness, yellowing skin, and bleeding. Victims of dengue fever suffer from headaches, painful joints, and a rash. In recent years, government programs have reduced the number of victims of these serious diseases.

Another insect is the termite, whose tall mounds—some as high as 5 feet (1.5 meters)—dot the savanna. Termites often destroy trees and wooden buildings and furniture.

Chapter 3

NATIVE KINGDOMS AND EUROPEAN EXPLORERS

More than ten thousand years ago many groups of people living in Africa lived in one place for a while and then moved on to other sites. This was true in what is now called Ivory Coast.

Although scientists have found much evidence of early human life in Africa, little is known about Ivory Coast's first people. However, bits and pieces of tools and weapons show that people lived throughout Ivory Coast during the Late Stone Age (8000 to 4000 B.C.). Ax heads and stones used to polish them have been found at Touba, Divo, Toumodi, Dimbokro, and Bouaké. Pieces of pottery have surfaced around Ferkéssédougou and Korhogo. The Bandama River and land around Abengourou have yielded other tools and weapons. By 1500 B.C., ancient Ivorians along the lagoons had built huge mounds of shells and broken pottery. The mounds served as burial places.

*Opposite page: A shell headdress worn by a young Senufo
girl from Boundiali for the traditional N'Goron dance*

Akan people live in Ivory Coast, as well as in nearby parts of Ghana. Traditional Akan dwellings (above) are round with thatch roofs. Akan basketmaking skills have been passed down through many generations (right).

Around A.D. 1, the area we presently call Ivory Coast already had become a meeting place for various African people. By that time, Mandé, Voltaic, Kru, and Akan languages could be heard in parts of Ivory Coast. Some researchers believe that about 250,000 people may have lived in the area by A.D. 200.

THE RISE AND FALL OF WEST AFRICAN EMPIRES

From about A.D. 400 to 1600, the empires of Ghana, Mali, and Songhai rose and fell on West Africa's savanna. They were located north of present-day Ivory Coast. Trade routes extending across the Sahara desert to North Africa crossed these savanna empires. The empires grew rich by taxing the imported salt and the exported gold and slaves carried by numerous trading caravans.

A small amount of gold came from goldfields in present-day Ivory Coast. The trade routes reached as far south as the northern edge of Ivory Coast's rain forest.

Many North African traders who traveled through the West African empires had converted to the religion of Islam. The Prophet Muhammad founded Islam in A.D. 622 in present-day Saudi Arabia. He preached about Allah, the one God. The Qur'an, or Koran, which contains revelations to Muhammad, is the Muslims' holy book.

From the tenth to the eighteenth centuries, West Africa's empires gradually came under Muslim influence. The Muslim traders established a separate town in Ghana's capital. Later, rulers of Mali and Songhai converted to Islam. Many West Africans, however, continued to follow their traditional local beliefs.

IVORY COAST'S KINGDOMS

Between the fourteenth and eighteenth centuries, several ethnic groups settled permanently in present-day Ivory Coast. The Senufo probably were one of the groups that entered Ivory Coast from the empire of Mali. They occupied the region lying between Odienné, Katiola, and Kong.

During the 1500s, the Mandé people from Mali also began moving south. As the Mandé pushed in, they squeezed the Senufo out of northwestern Ivory Coast. Muslim Mandé, called Dyula, also settled in the central and eastern stretches of the savanna. They occupied land in the kingdom of Kong. Agriculture, crafts, and trade flourished there. In Kong the Dyula traded salt from the Sahara and kola nuts from the rain forest. Under the Dyula, the

An Islamic mosque in what was the old kingdom of Kong in northern Ivory Coast

city of Kong became a great center of Islam. The Dyula built many beautiful mosques in which to pray. Some Dyula lived peacefully as traders and weavers among the Senufo.

People also began moving permanently into the eastern part of present-day Ivory Coast. Dyula traders arrived in Bondoukou in the 1500s. The city soon became a center of Muslim culture. Mosques were built, and Muslim scholars taught their religion in Qur'anic schools. In the 1600s, the Abron people from present-day Ghana settled south of Bondoukou. In time, Bondoukou became the center of the Abron Kingdom.

In the 1700s, the Baoulé and Agni broke off from the Ashanti, who controlled what is now western Ghana. The Baoulé pressed into the center of present-day Ivory Coast. Their kingdom lay south of the Kong Kingdom, between the Komoé and White Bandama Rivers. Sakasso was the Baoulé capital. The Baoulé Kingdom started out with a centralized government. After the rule of a few strong kings ended, the Baoulé separated into smaller chiefdoms. To the east the Agni set up the kingdoms of Indénié and Sanwi. Abengourou served as the capital of Indénié. Today, the Agni around Krinjabo still claim loyalty to a king. In 1959 and again in 1969, they attempted to break from Ivory Coast and form an independent kingdom.

While kingdoms grew in northern and eastern Ivory Coast, other ethnic groups became established in the western rain forest. The Dan lived at the northwestern edge of the rain forest. To the southwest were the Kru, Bete, and Guere. Many of these western people had come from what is now Liberia. These ethnic groups made their living by hunting and farming. These rain forest people purposely kept Dyula traders out of their territory. Instead, the rain forest dwellers themselves traded kola nuts from their forest for iron, desert salt, and other products.

In the lagoon area to the east, the Ébrié and the Abidji were the main groups. By 1600 about one million people lived in present-day Ivory Coast.

EUROPEAN EXPLORERS AND TRADERS

In the 1400s, Portuguese explorers and traders sought an ocean route to Asia. Their search brought them into the Gulf of Guinea. In 1469 Soerio da Costa, a Portuguese explorer, landed at Sassandra. Little is known about his contact there with Ivory Coast's Kru people.

For the next two hundred years, only a small amount of coastal trade took place. Rocks, rough surf, and sandbars made sea trade difficult. Because Ivory Coast had no natural harbors, Ivorians rowed large wooden boats carved from tree trunks out to meet European traders. Their boats were loaded with elephant tusks and gold. In Europe, ivory from the tusks was used to make piano

An old drawing of a load of ivory being carried toward the coast to be traded for goods brought by Europeans

keys, billiard balls, jewelry, and sculptures. In the early 1700s, the ivory trade had all but ended because few elephants were left.

A brisk trade in slaves also took place in the Gulf of Guinea. French, British, Dutch, and Portuguese traders bought African slaves to work on plantations in the American colonies. Trading of slaves among Africans had existed for centuries. However, those slaves could work their way out of slavery. They also could gain freedom by marrying a free person. But once an African was sold to a European slave trader, he or she would be a slave for life.

The slave trade never flourished in Ivory Coast as it did in Ghana and Nigeria. Nevertheless, in the early 1700s people from Ivory Coast were sold as slaves at coastal markets in Ghana. In the 1770s, slave trading also occurred at the mouth of the Bandama River west of Grand-Lahou. In exchange for African slaves, the European slavers brought new foods—maize and cassava—from the Americas.

A painting of a caravan of captives being taken to the coast to be sold as slaves and carried to the Americas

FRENCH SETTLEMENTS AND TRADE

The first European post in Ivory Coast was a French mission. Five Catholic missionaries established it in 1637 at Assini. Heat, humidity, and tropical diseases killed three of the men within a year. The other two went back to France. Fifty years later, a ship from the French navy stopped at Assini and took two young African men back to France. One of them, Aniaba, was a prince. He was educated and baptized a Catholic at the court of King Louis XIV. In 1701 Aniaba returned to Assini with missionaries and soldiers. They set up a military post. Three years later that settlement ended, once again because of the area's climate and diseases. By the 1700s, Europeans had nicknamed Ivory Coast "Bad Man's Coast." White men could not seem to survive there. Not until the 1800s did Frenchmen again set foot in this part of Africa.

From the 1840s through the 1860s, the French navy cruised in

The king of one of the many tribal groups within Ivory Coast, dressed for a wedding

the Gulf of Guinea along the Ivory Coast. French naval officers persuaded coastal chiefs from Assini, in the east, to Sassandra, in the west, to sign treaties with France. In the treaties, the chiefs agreed to trade only with the French and to allow the French to build forts and trading posts. France in turn agreed to pay the chiefs for use of the land.

The first French forts were built in 1842 and 1843 at Assini and Grand-Bassam. Soon after, trading posts went up next to the forts. During that time the first large amounts of palm oil were produced. Palm oil became an important export. In 1858 Arthur Verdier arrived to run the trading post at Grand-Bassam and was quite successful. The French government turned the other posts over to Verdier in 1871 and once again pulled out of Ivory Coast. At that time, France's government was weak. The country had just suffered a great defeat in a war with Prussia, a German state.

In the early 1880s, Verdier had villagers clear some jungle near Assini. In the clearing, Ivory Coast's first cocoa and coffee plantations were established. Verdier is believed to have obtained the plants from nearby Ghana. Also at that time, the first mahogany logs were exported from Ivory Coast.

THE RACE FOR AFRICA

Back in Europe, France and other countries began a great race to carve up Africa among themselves. At the Berlin Conference (1884–1885), they agreed that any country that wished to claim ownership over a part of Africa had to have government representatives there.

In 1886 the French government took back control of its coastal trading posts in Ivory Coast. From 1887 to 1889, two French explorers worked their way through Ivory Coast. Louis-Gustave Binger moved south to Kong. Marcel Treich-Laplène pushed north from Assini to Kong. Along the way they arranged protectorate treaties with local chiefs. Most of the chiefs hoped the French would help them in disputes with other groups. In the early 1890s, treaties were made with coastal chiefs from Grand-Lahou to Cavally. Once the treaties were in place, French troops built forts and posts. The treaties established France's claim to most of present-day Ivory Coast.

Mahogany trees, like this one, are used in making fine furniture.

Félix Houphouët-Boigny (at far left) at the official welcome for a French minister. Houphouët-Boigny was Ivory Coast's head of state throughout most of its existence as an independent nation.

Chapter 4

FROM FRENCH COLONY TO INDEPENDENT NATION

When the European countries had finished carving up Africa, only Liberia and Ethiopia were still independent countries. France controlled most of West Africa from the Mediterranean Sea to the Gulf of Guinea. England had most of East Africa from present-day Egypt to South Africa. Portugal, Belgium, Germany, and Italy ruled smaller areas throughout the continent.

The lands under European control became colonies. Almost every part of life in Africa was affected by this. Colonialism changed how Africans were ruled and how they made a living. It influenced their religions, languages, crafts, and family structures.

THE COLONY OF IVORY COAST

The French government officially proclaimed Ivory Coast a French colony in 1893 and named Louis-Gustave Binger as its governor. Ivory Coast's capital was at Grand-Bassam. In 1895 Ivory Coast became part of French West Africa, which also

The Governor's Palace is at Bingerville. This former capital was named for the first governor of the French colony, Louis-Gustave Binger.

included present-day Senegal, Guinea, Mali, Burkina Faso, Mauritania, Niger, and Benin. French West Africa had a governor-general in Senegal. He passed on France's orders to Ivory Coast's governor.

In 1899 a yellow fever epidemic spread through Grand-Bassam. More than two-thirds of the town's European population died. The following year the capital was moved to Bingerville, which had a healthier climate.

In the early years of colonial rule, Ivory Coast extended north only as far as Man in the west and Bondoukou and Bouna in the east. Land north of that was part of the colonies of French Sudan (present-day Mali) and Upper Volta (present-day Burkina Faso). In colonial Ivory Coast, the French had real control over only narrow strips of land along the coast and along the Komoé and southern Bandama Rivers. Treaties had never been made with most of the rain forest people, including the Baoulé, Dida, Bété, and Gouro.

RESISTANCE TO FRENCH RULE

One source of resistance to French rule was Samory Touré. He was a Malinké leader from Guinea. Between 1879 and 1898, Samory built a huge Muslim empire that covered large parts of West Africa. He built many mosques across this land and forced Islam on the people under his rule. In the northern part of present-day Ivory Coast, Samory controlled land between Odienné and Bouna. His capital was at Dabakala.

Samory's well-trained army resisted French attempts to push northward. When people in Kong sided with the French, Samory destroyed that town, even though it was a center of Islamic teaching. Some groups of Senufo supported Samory. He received weapons from the Baule. French forces finally captured Samory in 1898. He was trying to cross the mountains near Man as he fled back to Guinea. The French exiled Samory to Gabon, where he died in 1900.

Between 1902 and 1916, many groups of rain forest people led revolts against the French in Ivory Coast. At one time, in 1908, they forced the French back to a narrow strip along the coast. Under Governor Louis-Gabriel Angoulvant (1908–1916), French forces led harsh campaigns against the Baoulé,

A Baoulé wood carver's depiction of one of the many European invaders of his land

Dan, and Dida people. By 1916 Ivory Coast was firmly under the control of distant France.

IVORY COAST'S COLONIAL GOVERNMENT

Before colonization, present-day Ivory Coast had no central government. Local kings and village chiefs held power in small areas. The French, however, divided Ivory Coast into many districts that were governed by French district commanders. Village chiefs, or headmen, came under French control. In some villages, the district commanders appointed the chiefs. They were Ivorians who supported the French.

Ivorians became French subjects but not French citizens. This meant they had duties but no political rights. Ivorians who became educated and accepted French ways, however, could apply for French citizenship. As French subjects, Ivorians older than age ten had to pay a head tax. If they couldn't pay in cash, gold, ivory, or crops, adult Ivorians had to perform *corvée*—unpaid forced labor to build public works such as roads, canals, railroads, and wharves. Ivorian men had to serve in the French military. Ivorians also came under the *indigénat*, which gave French officials the power to deal out fines or jail sentences to Ivorians without first giving them a trial.

COLONIAL ECONOMY

Ivorians had a primarily subsistence economy in the years before colonization. They grew enough grain and vegetables for their villages. Many also engaged in trade. Under the French, large

French-owned plantations grew bananas (left) for export. The French also opened up the rain forest (right) by developing roads in the interior of the country.

amounts of new crops, such as cocoa, coffee, bananas, and pineapples, were grown on plantations. These cash crops became Ivory Coast's main exports. Most of the plantations were owned by French settlers. Ivorians were used as corvée on the French plantations. A few Ivorians also started plantations but found it hard to compete with the French settlers. Ivorian planters could not use corvée and were sometimes themselves forced to work on French plantations.

Between 1901 and 1934, Ivory Coast changed in many other ways under French rule. Wharves were constructed at Grand-Bassam to make it easier to export coffee, cocoa, rubber, and timber. The Asagny Canal was built to connect the port of Grand-Lahou with Abidjan and Grand-Bassam. Railroad track was laid between Abidjan and Bobo-Dioulasso in Burkina Faso. A network of roads was built in the interior. In 1934 Abidjan became Ivory Coast's new capital.

The corvée supplied most of the workers for these projects. To be sure there were enough workers, the French moved whole villages closer to the transportation routes. Even then, Ivory Coast's population could not furnish enough men for those projects, so the French brought in corvée workers from Burkina Faso.

SOCIAL AND CULTURAL EFFECTS OF COLONIALISM

France brought its culture to Ivory Coast. All official business in Ivory Coast was done in the French language, according to French laws and customs, and with French money. Ivorian languages and customs were not prohibited, as long as they didn't get in the way of France's goals for the colony.

Catholic and Protestant missionaries entered Ivory Coast. They converted some Ivorians to Christianity. Catholic missionaries set up some primary schools and a few secondary schools where students learned to read, write, and speak French. The main purpose of the schools was to train Ivorians to become clerks and translators in the colonial government. Some Ivorians were sent to France or Senegal for higher education. Educated Ivorians were appointed to positions once held by chiefs. Sometimes this caused rivalries between traditional chiefs and westernized Ivorians.

Two new classes of Ivorians developed, Ivorian planters and Ivorian civil servants. The planters owned their plantations and made money from cash crops. The planters could afford to send their children to secondary school and even to college. Those

Even today, French remains the primary language of business and government in Ivory Coast. Many other languages are used in the interior.

educated Ivorians received positions in the colonial government. Most of them lived in Abidjan or other Ivorian cities. A gap had been created between urban and rural Ivorians and between Ivorian planters and village farmers.

IVORY COAST'S ROLE IN WORLD WAR I AND II

France was still working to bring Ivory Coast under its control when, in 1914, World War I broke out in Europe. To help with the war effort, Ivory Coast's planters and farmers had to produce larger amounts of cocoa, cotton, rice, and rubber. Almost twenty thousand Ivorians were drafted into the French army. Many of them were shipped to France. Other Ivorians refused to be drafted. The draft, war-related taxes, and increased production for the war effort caused a revolt in Ivory Coast, which the colonial government forcibly ended. When World War I ended in 1918, most Ivorian soldiers returned to their villages, but a number of men moved to Ivorian cities.

In the 1920s, Ivorians exported hardwood logs . This old photograph shows them floating logs through the surf to a ship, where they were winched aboard.

The end of the war brought more French settlers to Ivory Coast. Many were laborers who hoped to strike it rich. Some set up businesses in the coastal cities, while others started plantations. In general, these new French settlers had racist attitudes toward the Ivorians. They set up social clubs that were open only to Europeans.

In 1936 a socialist government came to power in France. Its leaders were more understanding of Ivorian needs. They passed regulations that raised the minimum wage and reduced the amount of time spent on the corvée. Some Ivorians set up the Socialist Party of the Ivory Coast.

Relaxed conditions ended with the coming of World War II in 1939. France fell to Nazi Germany in 1940. When the pro-Nazi Vichy government rose to power in France, the colonial governors sided with the Vichy government. The corvée was extended, and Ivorians were discriminated against because of their race. When General Charles de Gaulle took leadership of the Free French government, Ivorians supported him. The king of Bondoukou fled

French war hero Charles de Gaulle, speaking in 1944

to Ghana to help de Gaulle. Village chiefs led resistance movements to sabotage the Vichy war effort.

In 1943 André Latrille, a de Gaulle supporter, was named governor of Ivory Coast. A year later he approved the founding of the *Syndicat Agricole Africain* (African Agricultural Union) (SAA). The SAA was led by Félix Houphouët-Boigny and other Ivorian planters. They wanted to end the corvée and improve the position of Ivorian planters and farmers. Up to that time, French planters received higher prices for their crops than Ivorian planters did, and they also were able to get their crops to market more easily. By 1945 the SAA had twenty thousand members. They included planters, small farmers, traders, and laborers from all ethnic groups and areas of Ivory Coast.

POSTWAR REFORMS

Although France was one of the victors in World War II, it was a much poorer country in 1945. The French government began to consider different ways to rule its colonies. In October 1945, France allowed Ivory Coast's first election. Two delegates were elected to the Constituent Assembly in Paris. One was elected by the French settlers. Houphouët-Boigny was the other delegate.

Houphouët-Boigny sponsored a bill to end the corvée. It easily passed and made him a hero throughout all of French West Africa. The Constituent Assembly passed many other reforms. French citizenship was given to all people in France's colonies. With citizenship came freedom of speech and assembly, although not all citizens had the right to vote. The indigénat was abolished so all West Africans were afforded the protection of French law and a court trial. The delegates also agreed to improve the colonies' schools, hospitals, and clinics.

In April 1946, Houphouët-Boigny returned to Ivory Coast. He founded the *Parti Démocratique de la Côte d'Ivoire* (Democratic Party of the Ivory Coast) (PDCI). As a member of the PDCI, Houphouët-Boigny was reelected as a delegate to the Second Constituent Assembly. That assembly formed the French Union, which included France and its territories. Ivory Coast became an overseas territory with a Territorial Assembly and the Municipal Council of Abidjan, but regulations still came from Paris. Houphouët-Boigny and other West Africans were disappointed that they had not won local self-government.

THE RISE OF HOUPHOUËT-BOIGNY

Houphouët-Boigny had a wide power base. He was a doctor, a planter, and a Baoulé chief. Born in 1905, in Yamoussoukro, Houphouët-Boigny was a member of the Baule, Ivory Coast's largest ethnic group. At the age of eleven, he became a Catholic. When Houphouët-Boigny had received as much education as Ivory Coast had to offer, he entered the École Ponty in Senegal for training as a doctor. From 1925 to 1940, he served at many medical posts in southeastern Ivory Coast. There he married a woman related to the Agni kings. His marriage gave him kinship ties with another large ethnic group. In the southeast, Houphouët-Boigny

Photo taken in 1956 of Félix Houphouët-Boigny in France, just after Charles de Gaulle named him to the French cabinet

met many Ivorian planters and learned of the problems they faced in competing with the French planters.

In 1940, Houphouët-Boigny inherited coffee and cocoa lands near Yamoussoukro and returned home to manage the plantations. Soon after, he was appointed chief for that area. Houphouët-Boigny used his position to form the Association of Customary Chiefs. Through this organization, he became well known and respected by chiefs throughout Ivory Coast. Between 1944 and 1946, he founded the PDCI and the *Rassemblement Démocratique Africain,* (African Democratic Rally) (RDA). The RDA was made up of members from political parties throughout French West Africa.

From 1946 to 1959, Houphouët-Boigny served as Ivory Coast's representative to the French National Assembly. In 1956 he was appointed as a minister in the French government and became mayor of Abidjan. In 1957 he was elected president of both the Grand Council of French West Africa in Senegal and the Territorial Assembly of the Ivory Coast. Houphouët-Boigny thus had great political influence, not only in Ivory Coast but also throughout West Africa and as far away as France.

One of the first projects of an independent Ivory Coast was the development of a telephone system connecting all the major cities.

THE ROAD TO INDEPENDENCE

By the mid-1950s, Ivory Coast had already become French West Africa's most prosperous territory. Almost one-half of French West Africa's exports came from Ivory Coast, and almost one-third of the region's imports entered through Ivory Coast. The completion of the Vridi Canal in 1950 opened Abidjan to oceangoing ships and greatly aided Ivory Coast's role in trade. Independence from France was not yet an issue. Ivorian leaders continued to work for more control over local government and for full equality within the French Union.

In 1956 the French government passed more reforms for its territories. All adults in Ivory Coast received the right to vote.

They could elect representatives to local and district councils. The Territorial Assembly could make laws for Ivory Coast.

Two years later, Charles de Gaulle became president of France. Through his work, the French Community was created. Each French territory could vote on becoming a member and then form its own government and write a constitution. Under the French Community, France still controlled economic, foreign, and defense policies. In September 1958, Ivory Coast voted to become a self-governing republic in the French Community. Six months later, Ivorians adopted their first constitution. In an election in April 1959, members of the PDCI won all the seats in Ivory Coast's new legislature, which elected Houphouët-Boigny as prime minister.

Houphouët-Boigny also continued in his role as regional leader. Later in 1959, he and other West African leaders formed the Council of Entente. Through that organization, they made plans for the region's economic growth.

In 1960 the French government made it possible for members of the French Community to become independent nations and still

Charles de Gaulle, president of France, visited Abidjan in 1958 as Ivory Coast was preparing to become a self-governing republic.

remain members of the French Community. On August 7, 1960, Ivory Coast proclaimed its independence and withdrew from the organization. However, the new nation decided to maintain its trade relations with France and to keep many French professionals and government advisers. In October 1960, Ivory Coast's National Assembly adopted a new constitution and elected Houphouët-Boigny as president of the new independent republic.

PERSONAL, ONE-MAN, ONE-PARTY RULE

From the early months of independence, the stamp of Houphouët-Boigny's personal power was imprinted on Ivory Coast. He used his personal charisma and his broad political base to unify Ivory Coast's many ethnic groups. Houphouët-Boigny used the Ivorian custom of the *palaver,* a discussion about disagreements, to help him govern. After villagers talked together about problems, Ivorian chiefs would make a decision. For his palavers, Houphouët-Boigny brought people from all over Ivory Coast to Abidjan, let them talk about problems facing the country, and then proclaimed new policies.

Much like a United States president, Houphouët-Boigny was head of government, head of state, and commander-in-chief of the armed forces. He also was head of Ivory Coast's only legal political party, the PDCI. In the years after independence, only PDCI members could be elected to office. Only those publications that were approved by the government or PDCI were available to Ivorians. Freedom of speech and of the press did not exist.

Not all Ivorians went along with governmental and PDCI policies. In the 1960s, those dissenters were quickly rounded up

With independence, small native planters such as this cocoa grower (left) began to play a larger role in production of this important export crop. The man on the right is monitoring the humidity level of stored cocoa.

and arrested. If they admitted their guilt, Houphouët-Boigny pardoned them. Others, especially students, were forced into military service. In that way, Houphouët-Boigny could say that Ivory Coast held no political prisoners. Houphouët-Boigny justified his actions on the grounds that political stability was required to achieve economic prosperity.

Houphouët-Boigny encouraged planters and businesspeople to run for local and national offices. In that way, Ivory Coast was governed by people who had an economic interest in maintaining a stable government. By 1990 about 25 percent of the country's mayors were businesspeople or came from business families. About 35 percent of the National Assembly's deputies had business backgrounds, although businesspeople made up only 1 percent of Ivory Coast's population.

Houphouët-Boigny also introduced the policy of Ivoirization, under which trained and educated Ivorians gradually began

Houphouët-Boigny (at center) at age 85, campaigning in the 1990 election

replacing French government advisers, teachers, technicians, and managers. However, Ivoirization has not happened fast enough to suit many Ivorians.

Perhaps Houphouët-Boigny's greatest achievement was making Ivory Coast the wealthiest country in West Africa. Because Ivory Coast had limited resources at independence, he wanted Ivorians to concentrate on increasing agricultural output. On the other hand, he encouraged foreign companies to invest in Ivorian industries and to build factories. During the first eight years of independence, coffee, cocoa, and banana production increased by 50 percent and pineapple production by 200 percent. By 1980 the per capita income had increased 61 percent. This new wealth was more evenly distributed among Ivory Coast's population than was the case in other African countries.

ECONOMIC PROBLEMS BRING POLITICAL CHANGES

In the late 1970s, cocoa and coffee prices fell. Farmers and planters received lower prices for their crops. In the early 1980s several years of severe drought lowered the size and quality of the rice and millet crops. Many farmers, hard hit by poverty, moved to the cities to find work. Although Ivory Coast still was better off than most other African countries, the gap between rich Ivorians and poor Ivorians had grown. The cities became overcrowded. Wealthy foreigners and Ivorians became targets of urban criminals.

The government looked to the World Bank and the International Monetary Fund (IMF) for aid. To qualify for loans, the IMF required reforms in Ivory Coast. The government had to cut back on civil service pay and reduce the number of grants to secondary and college students. Discontent grew among most classes of Ivorians. Rumors of corruption at high levels of government spread. Many Ivorians called for an end to one-party rule, and some even talked of ousting Houphouët-Boigny from power.

Throughout 1990, students, health-care workers, soldiers, bus drivers, financial workers, and others held strikes or demonstrations. Abidjan's electrical power was prone to sudden and long shutdowns. Even Abidjan's Roman Catholic Cardinal Bernard Yago called on the government to relieve the poor from more hardships.

In response to the unrest, Houphouët-Boigny legalized nine political parties and allowed publication of an opposition

Supporters of Laurent Gbagbo campaigning in the 1990 election, Ivory Coast's first multiparty election

newspaper. He appointed Alassane Ouattara, who had previously worked with the IMF, to work out a plan for true economic reform and recovery.

In the fall of 1990, Ivory Coast's first multiparty elections were held. In October Houphouët-Boigny received 85 percent of the vote for a seventh term as president. Laurent Gbagbo was the opposition candidate from the Ivorian Popular Front Party. In the November elections for the National Assembly, Gbagbo won 1 of 12 seats that went to opposition candidates. The PDCI maintained a wide majority—163 seats. The opposition made charges that voting was rigged and that people had voted more than once.

A constitutional amendment also was passed in November. Under this amendment, the leader of the National Assembly would become president on the death or resignation of Houphouët-Boigny. Henri Konan Bédié, National Assembly leader, was regarded as Houphouët-Boigny's successor. Like Houphouët-Boigny, Konan Bédié was a Catholic Baule. Another amendment

Henri Konan Bédié (right) became president after Houphouët-Boigny's death in 1993. He is shown here in 1995 with French president Jacques Chirac in Yamoussoukro.

provided for appointment of a prime minister. Alassane Ouattara, a Muslim, was named prime minister.

THE END OF AN ERA

On December 7, 1993, Houphouët-Boigny died. A short struggle for power took place between Ouattara and Konan Bédié. France, the United States, and other countries backed Konan Bédié's constitutional claim to power. Within twenty-four hours, Ouattara and his supporters had stepped aside.

Konan Bédié does not enjoy the popularity and power base Houphouët-Boigny did—no one could. The Ivorian people have been toughened by the hardships of the 1980s and early 1990s. They now expect to play a greater role in deciding Ivory Coast's political and economic goals. They will support leaders who encourage personal freedom and who continue to make economic reforms.

Chapter 5

STABILITY, PROGRESS, AND COMPROMISE

Since becoming independent in 1960, Ivory Coast's government has worked to maintain a stable environment that promotes economic growth. This sometimes has been done at the expense of the people's personal freedom, however. The government has expanded the health care and educational systems to reach more Ivorians. Nevertheless, during hard economic times poor and rural Ivorians have suffered from cutbacks in health care and education.

CONSTITUTIONAL GOVERNMENT

Ivory Coast's present constitution was adopted in 1960. Many amendments have been added to it since then. Based on the French constitution of 1958, it established a democratic republic with three branches of government. The executive, legislative, and judicial branches have separate but unequal powers.

The executive branch is meant to exercise the most power in Ivory Coast's government. It is headed by a president who is elected directly by the people every five years. The president's powers include appointing and removing government ministers,

This Ivorian boy will have more opportunities to become involved with the governing of his country than his parents and grandparents did.

judges, and military leaders; suggesting new laws; carrying out laws; and negotiating treaties with other countries. Helping the president are the Council of Ministers and the Economic and Social Council. Members of the councils can suggest ideas, laws, or programs to the president.

The legislative branch is made up of the National Assembly. Since 1985 the National Assembly has consisted of 175 deputies who are elected for five-year terms. Each deputy comes from a separate district. The deputies then elect a leader, or speaker, of the National Assembly. Should the president die or resign, that person will take over as president of Ivory Coast. The deputies pass or reject laws suggested by the president. They also may decide on

Troops patrolled the streets of Abidjan to stop disturbances during the first multiparty elections, held in Ivory Coast in 1990.

laws introduced by other deputies. Since 1960 all of Ivory Coast's laws have come from the president.

The judicial branch is made up of lower and superior courts. The lower courts hear all levels of criminal and civil cases, as well as the appeals of those cases. The superior courts include the Supreme Court, High Court of Justice, and the State Security Court. One section of the Supreme Court reviews laws passed by the National Assembly before they are put into effect. The High Court of Justice can impeach the president and try other government officers if they have committed crimes while in office. Ivory Coast's president has final appointment of the judges in all those courts.

In addition to the national government, Ivory Coast has several layers of local government. The country is divided into forty-nine prefectures, each headed by a prefect. The prefectures are further divided into subprefectures headed by a subprefect. Prefects and subprefects are appointed from Abidjan and usually aren't from the area they govern. The duties of prefects and subprefects are to see that all laws are carried out and that government services such as health care, education, and information for farmers reach the right people.

Villages and cities also have governments. Each village in Ivory Coast selects a leader, or chief. The prefect must approve these selections. The village chiefs then come under the supervision of the subprefects. Thirty-seven of Ivory Coast's cities have municipal councils elected by the citizens. Each council elects a mayor. The municipal councils and mayors usually follow guidelines sent from the minister of the interior.

Ivory Coast's constitution allows for political parties. In 1990 candidates from twenty-six political parties ran for the National Assembly. All citizens over twenty-one years of age have the right to vote in Ivory Coast, but only 40 percent cast ballots.

CIVIL RIGHTS

Ivory Coast's constitution states that the power of the government comes from the people. The constitution guarantees all people equal treatment before the law without regard to religion, race, gender, or place of birth. As in the United States, Ivorians are presumed innocent until proved guilty and have the right to have a lawyer represent them in court. However, the right to post bail is not guaranteed. That is why Ivorians sometimes stay in jail from the time they are arrested until their trial is over.

The Ivorian constitution also guarantees freedom of religion and freedom from racial discrimination. Freedom of the press and freedom of assembly, however, are not guaranteed in the Ivorian constitution. Other rights, such as freedom of speech, are left for the National Assembly to approve. By placing limits on freedom of the press, assembly, and speech, the government is more easily able to control the people. In recent years, the government has allowed some opposition newspapers to be published. They present the views of the newly legalized opposition political parties.

INTERNATIONAL RELATIONS

Since independence, Ivory Coast's main policy in international relations has been cooperation. By following that policy, Ivory Coast has not had to build up a large military force. In 1959, before achieving independence, Ivory Coast founded the Council of Entente with Burkina Faso, Benin, and Niger. Through this council, which now also includes Togo, each member country has direct ties to France and French economic aid. Ivory Coast is also a member of the Organization of African Unity (OAU). In the 1970s, Ivory Coast joined the Economic Community of West African States (ECOWAS). The ECOWAS works to keep peace and to encourage freer flow of trade among member countries.

Ivory Coast's relations with its immediate neighbors—Ghana, Liberia, Guinea, Mali, and Burkina Faso—have changed over the years, depending on their governments. In 1985 Houphouët-Boigny helped negotiate peace between Mali and Burkina Faso over a border disagreement. In 1989 Ivory Coast became involved in Liberia's civil war, started by Charles Taylor. In 1991 Houphouët-Boigny hosted a peace conference in Yamoussoukro between Taylor and the Liberian government.

Ivory Coast's foreign policy in regard to the rest of the world

Charles Taylor, a Liberian rebel, started a civil war in Liberia. He led his forces into Liberia from Ivory Coast. Many African leaders believed that weapons reached Taylor's army through Ivory Coast. When Liberian refugees fled to Ivory Coast, refugee camps were set up near Danané and Zouan-Hounien.

has sometimes gone against the thinking of other African countries. During the Nigerian Civil War (1966–1971), Ivory Coast was one of only four African countries to side with the Biafrans in their attempt to set up an independent state. In the 1970s, Houphouët-Boigny started talks with South Africa and allowed some South African goods into the country. At that time, South Africa practiced *apartheid*, separation of the races. The rest of black Africa refused to have any open dealings with South Africa.

In the early 1960s, Ivory Coast and Israel opened diplomatic relations. Israeli experts provided advice for building up Ivory Coast's banking system, agriculture, and tourism. Under pressure from other African countries, Ivory Coast broke diplomatic relations with Israel in 1973. However, the two countries continued to maintain informal economic relations. In 1986 Ivory Coast resumed full diplomatic relations with Israel.

Ivory Coast has maintained a close relationship with the United States. Houphouët-Boigny took pride in his many trips to the United States and his meetings with eight American presidents, from Dwight Eisenhower to George Bush. A lively cultural exchange program has been carried out between American and Ivorian government officials, businesspeople, teachers, and students. The United States has given much aid to the Ivory Coast for energy, health care, and loan programs.

Ivory Coast's closest ties, of course, are with France. French troops are stationed near Abidjan for Ivory Coast's security. France remains Ivory Coast's number-one trading partner. Ivory Coast continues to receive French economic aid.

EDUCATION

Ivory Coast's education system is based on the French system that was started during colonial times. Since independence, educational services have been expanded to reach more people. However, there are no laws that require Ivorians to attend school for a certain number of years. Families tend to send their sons rather than their daughters to school. That is why the literacy rate for men in 1990 was about 55 percent, whereas for women it was only about 35 percent. The overall literacy rate was 45 percent.

There are three levels of public education in Ivory Coast—primary, secondary, and higher education. Instruction is given in French at all levels. Most textbooks are still published in France, although Ivory Coast started producing some texts in the 1980s. The Ivorian books reflect African values and culture.

About 75 percent of Ivorian boys and 50 percent of girls attend primary school. Many of the schools are overcrowded and cannot accept all the students who want to attend. Most primary teachers are Ivorians. Children do not begin primary school until they are seven or eight years old. There, they master the French language.

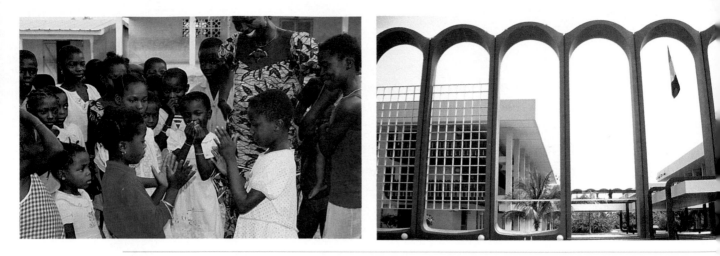

Children playing a singing and clapping game at primary school (left), and a branch of the National University of Côte d'Ivoire at Yamoussoukro (right)

Over six years, primary-school students have classes in reading, writing, arithmetic, natural sciences, history, geography, art, music, and physical education. In village schools the children also learn farming methods by working in the schools' vegetable gardens.

Only about 20 percent of primary-school graduates go on to secondary school, and many of them drop out before completing the full seven years. Secondary schools are located in large towns or cities, and many village families cannot afford the transportation and housing costs involved in sending children to secondary schools. Those who attend secondary school can train to become teachers, receive vocational training, or prepare to enter university. An Ivorian secondary-school graduate has about the same level of education as a person in the United States with one or two years of college.

The National University of Ivory Coast in Abidjan is the country's major university. Many professors and instructors are French. About twenty thousand students are enrolled here. Almost half of them are from other African countries. Less than four thousand women attend. A few thousand Ivorians also attend universities in France, the United States, Canada, and Belgium.

In addition to the government-run schools and universities, there are several Catholic primary and secondary schools. Most of them are in the southeastern part of the country. In the more heavily Muslim north, Qur'anic schools teach about Islam. Some Muslim students also attend public schools or Catholic schools. As long as the Catholic schools follow the same program as the public schools and do not require that students learn about Catholicism, the Ivorian government pays part of the teachers' salaries. Muslim schools, however, do not receive government funds because they emphasize religious instruction. Adult education in Ivory Coast's cities is limited to night courses.

HEALTH

Since gaining independence, the health of Ivorians has greatly improved. In 1960 the average Ivorian lived to be thirty-nine years old. By 1992 the average was fifty-three years for men and fifty-seven for women. These ages are much higher than those in most other African countries. Within Ivory Coast itself, southern villagers have a longer life span. As with education, the quality and quantity of health care are not the same for all Ivorians.

In poor sections of the cities, overcrowding and inadequate water and sewerage facilities cause health problems. Rural Ivorians totally lack running water and safe ways to dispose of waste. Also, malnutrition is higher in rural areas. Between harvests, villagers often run out of surplus food. The death rate of

Left: As part of a UNICEF program, this woman is growing healthful vegetables in her garden. Above: A biologist looks for blackfly larvae in a disease-monitoring program.

young children and the elderly is especially high at these times.

Poor sanitation and nutrition have led to Ivorians being susceptible to many diseases. The Ivorian government, the World Health Organization (WHO), and the United Nations Children's Fund (UNICEF) have provided vaccination programs against yellow fever, tetanus, polio, tuberculosis, measles, and diphtheria. Many Ivorians also suffer from diseases caused by mosquitoes and other parasites, such as malaria, hookworm, yaws, and onchocerciasis, which causes blindness.

By the 1990s, AIDS was the leading cause of death in Abidjan. The government has started blood-screening programs to determine carriers of that disease. It also began providing Ivorians with information about AIDS.

The Ivorian government has spent large amounts of money to build hospitals and to train doctors and nurses. It has encouraged the growth of private hospitals and clinics. Most of those health care centers, however, are in the cities and larger rural towns. Villagers have difficulty reaching medical help. If villagers do get to a clinic or hospital, they usually have a long wait because of the shortage of doctors and nurses. Often, the necessary medicine or equipment is not available.

Chapter 6

REBUILDING THE IVORIAN MIRACLE

During the first twenty years of its independence, Ivory Coast enjoyed great economic success. Prices for exports of cocoa, coffee, and timber remained high. Increased yields of bananas, pineapple, cotton, sugarcane, rubber, and palm oil added to the country's wealth. Money from those agricultural goods was used to build dams and ports, to improve the roads and railroad, and to expand the education and health care systems. Oil was found offshore from Abidjan and Grand-Bassam. Industries owned by French companies began producing manufactured goods. Other industries were jointly owned by the Ivorian government and Ivorian businesspeople. This steady economic growth was proudly proclaimed the "Ivorian miracle."

ECONOMIC SETBACKS

By the 1980s, Ivory Coast's economy had begun to falter. Too much cocoa and coffee were being produced around the world, so

Opposite page: One of the many oil palm plantations that provide the palm oil long used for cooking throughout the world

Most major industry is in or near Abidjan. Petroleum products are stored in a factory area (above). Not very far away is the modern bank building of La Société Ivoirienne de Banque *(right).*

their prices fell. Timber production decreased because few trees were left. The demand for palm oil lessened as American and European baking companies stopped using it in their cakes and cookies because palm oil, which is high in saturated fats, had been linked to heart disease. In addition, droughts on the savanna throughout the 1980s hurt the cotton crop as well as the food crops for local villages. With less money from exports, Ivory Coast began borrowing money from other countries to continue the growth of its industries and social programs. When interest rates shot up, Ivory Coast could not repay its loans and sank deeper in debt.

In the late 1980s and early 1990s, measures were taken to depend less on agricultural exports and to encourage more production of Ivorian manufactured products. The government has worked with the International Monetary Fund and World Bank to arrange payments on Ivory Coast's $18-billion debt. The government has pulled out of many industries, turning control over to private individuals. If these measures work, the end of the twentieth century could see the return of the Ivorian miracle.

AGRICULTURE

Agriculture remains the largest part of Ivory Coast's economy. About 60 percent of the people use 50 percent of the land for farming. Plantations are owned by companies and wealthy families, who hire Ivorian villagers and farmers from neighboring countries to plant and harvest the crops. On a few of the larger plantations, workers operate tractors and threshers.

In Ivorian villages, individual farmers work fields of varying sizes. Village farmers do their work by hand with the same kinds of tools that have been used for hundreds of years. They use a long cutting knife to clear the fields and a hoe, called a *daba*, to till the soil.

Two types of crops are raised in Ivory Coast—commercial crops and food crops. Commercial crops are grown for export or for further processing in Ivory Coast. Those crops include cocoa, coffee, rubber, pineapples, bananas, palm oil fruit, coconuts, cotton, and sugarcane. Ivory Coast leads the world in cocoa bean production and is third in producing coffee beans. Most commercial crops are raised on plantations. However, more village farmers now have set aside large plots of land for cotton, coffee, and cocoa.

Food crops are grown in fields and vegetable gardens by individual families. Crops grown in fields include yams, plantain (a bananalike fruit), cassava and taro (plants whose roots are used for food), rice, maize (corn), and sorghum and millet (grains). Individual families also raise beans, peas, tomatoes, eggplant, and okra in vegetable gardens. Sometimes these vegetables are planted between rows of field crops.

Bush fallow, or shifting agriculture, is practiced in most

Scenes from Ivory Coast's agricultural life include (clockwise from top left): the open market in Abidjan selling produce from small farms; a rice plantation; harvesting coffee beans; and loading goats for market.

Crops may be grown for personal use, like these yams drying for storage (above), or for the commercial market. This raw cotton (right) is ready for shipping.

villages. A field is cultivated for three or four years and then left unplanted for up to ten years. In some rotations, yams are planted during the first year; maize, the second; and cassava, the third. Other rotations include cotton and rice. As farmers felt more pressure to grow more food, they began to leave fields fallow for shorter periods of time. That practice has caused the soil to lose more nutrients, resulting in smaller crop yields.

Little livestock is raised in Ivory Coast. Most of the cattle are raised by Fulani herders who roam across the northern savanna. Many cattle fall victim to the tsetse fly. Frequent droughts have led to sparse grasslands for those herds. For those reasons Ivory Coast's cattle do not have as much meat on them as American beef cattle. In recent years, feed lots have been set up near Abidjan and Bouaké to help fatten the cattle. Individual families raise pigs, sheep, goats, and chickens, mainly for their own use. Some farmers sell eggs and chickens in the city markets.

FISHING AND FORESTRY

Ivorians who live on the coast or near the country's rivers and lakes add to their diets and income by catching fish. Tuna and sardines are caught in nets from large fishing ships in the Gulf of

Left: Fishermen in Abidjan harbor mending their nets
Right: Men and large machines handling hardwood logs from Ivory Coast's forests

Guinea. Many lagoon fishermen use canoes with outboard motors. They trap such crustaceans as shrimp and crabs in pots. Each morning, shrimp and crab fishermen take their boats out to check their catches. Close to shore, women gather shrimp and crabs by hand. Some fishermen on the lagoons and rivers throw nets from shore into the water with a big circular motion. Then they pull in the nets filled with fish. River fishermen also set traps or use spears or hooks and lines. In recent years, Ivory Coast's artificial lakes and ponds have been stocked with fish. Much of the catch is eaten fresh near where it was caught. Some is dried or smoked for shipping within Ivory Coast and to nearby African countries. Recently, tuna, sardine, and shrimp canneries have been built in Abidjan. Most canned fish is shipped to European countries.

Forestry has declined greatly in Ivory Coast. The rain forest has been overcut, and replanting programs have not progressed as planned. Small amounts of mahogany, samba, and sau trees are still felled, with some used for Ivorian ceremonial masks, furniture, plywood, and prefabricated houses. Whole logs and timber sawed at local mills are shipped to other African countries and to Europe.

A pipeline being built through the rain forest

MINING

Ivory Coast has a limited amount of mineral resources. Many of them, such as gold and iron ore, are of low quality and are hard to reach. Ivory Coast also has small deposits of bauxite, cobalt, copper, diamonds, manganese, and nickel.

Two small oil fields were discovered in deep water in the Gulf of Guinea in the 1970s. Phillips Petroleum and Exxon, two United States companies, drilled wells in those oil fields. By the early 1980s, each of the fields was producing between 10,000 and 20,000 barrels per day. When the worldwide price of oil dropped in the mid-1980s, however, it became too expensive to continue working the fields and the oil wells were capped.

Large natural gas fields were found near the oil fields. Ivory Coast hopes to use the gas to generate electricity at the Vridi power station. A by-product of the gas could be used to make fertilizer, which would greatly improve Ivory Coast's agriculture. But the gas wells have yet to be drilled. The cost of drilling and of building a pipeline to Vridi will be close to $200 million.

MANUFACTURING

Manufacturing in Ivory Coast has changed greatly since 1960. In 1992 about 10 percent of the labor force was employed in manufacturing. That number was up 6 percent from 1960. About 20 percent of today's labor force comes from other African countries. In 1960 there were only fifty manufacturing companies in Ivory Coast. Most of them were European owned. By the 1990s, there were more than six hundred manufacturing companies, many of them Ivorian owned and managed.

In the colonial years, Ivory Coast's factories made food products, wood products, and cloth from locally grown materials. In addition to those goods, today's Ivorian factories import raw materials to produce metals, heavy equipment, and chemicals. Abidjan and Bouaké remain the centers of Ivory Coast's industry. However, factories have sprung up in San Pédro, Daloa, Agboville, Danané, Abengourou, Dabou, Bouaflé, Man, Gagnoa, and Diva.

Food products continue to head the list of Ivorian products. They include processed coffee and cocoa beans and processed coconut and palm oil. Beverages such as malt drinks, soft drinks, beer, pineapple juice, and bottled water are other important products. Ice cream, sweetened condensed milk, and chocolate are a few newer foods produced in the country. Canned pineapple slices, tuna, sardines, and shrimp are Ivory Coast's leading exports of ready-to-eat foods.

Textiles and clothing made in Ivory Coast range from cotton thread and cloth to material for *pagnes* (several yards of hand-woven or machine-woven cloth that is wrapped and folded around the body) to ready-to-wear clothing. Companies making

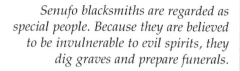

Senufo blacksmiths are regarded as special people. Because they are believed to be invulnerable to evil spirits, they dig graves and prepare funerals.

building materials such as cement, corrugated-steel roofing, lumber, and plywood have prospered. In the 1980s, the government started to encourage villagers to construct their homes with those materials rather than mud bricks and thatch.

Heavy industries have recently expanded in Ivory Coast. Air conditioners, freezers, and refrigerators—much needed in a hot, humid climate—now are made locally. Ivorian factories make chemicals such as glue, paint, varnish, ink, pesticides, and medicines. Crude oil from Nigeria is refined at Vridi. Railroad cars and heavy metals such as steel are other Ivorian products. Although Ivory Coast's manufacturing has greatly increased, the country still relies on many imports.

INTERNATIONAL TRADE AND TOURISM

Ivory Coast has limited amounts of natural resources, has difficulty growing enough food for its people, and is still building up its manufacturing companies. For those reasons, trade with other countries plays an important role in the economy. Ivorians have developed tastes for bread and beer. To make those items, they must import wheat flour, wheat, and other grains. More than 60 percent of the country's beef is imported from Europe, Burkina

Faso, and Mali. More than 100,000 tons of frozen fish are shipped to Ivory Coast each year. Ivorians rely on other countries for most of their milk.

Automobiles, buses, and trucks, as well as parts to keep those machines running are shipped from Japan and Europe. Ivory Coast also imports its tractors, bulldozers, and other heavy equipment. All of lvory Coast's crude oil is imported, as are most of the supplies needed for its chemical industry.

To pay for those imported goods, Ivory Coast exports its leading products, including cocoa beans and processed cocoa, coffee beans and processed coffee, canned fish, wood, and refined oil. Ivory Coast's exports go mainly to France, the Netherlands,

The newest industry in Ivory Coast is tourism. This is a new resort hotel in Yamoussoukro.

Cargo ships docked in the port of Abidjan

Germany, Italy, Belgium, and the United States. Burkina Faso, Mali, and Nigeria are its biggest markets in Africa.

In recent years, the government has promoted tourism, mainly to Europeans. They are invited to enjoy the cultural heritages of sixty different ethnic groups, wild animal reserves and parks, and the surf and white beaches. In 1991 tourists spent more than $46 million in Ivory Coast.

TRANSPORTATION AND COMMUNICATION

Trade and tourism have made Abidjan the busiest seaport in West Africa. Abidjan's docks serve passenger ships, oil tankers and other cargo ships, and the boats and canoes of local fishermen. San Pédro is Ivory Coast's second-largest port. The docks at those two ports employ thousands of workers who load and unload the ships. Close to the docks, warehouses store millions of tons of goods awaiting shipment into or out of the country.

The Houphouët-Boigny Bridge in Abidjan has more car traffic than almost any other place in Ivory Coast. There are few private cars outside the big cities.

To move goods and people around the country, Ivory Coast has 42,250 miles (68,000 kilometers) of roads. About 8 percent of those roads are paved with blacktop. The road between Abidjan and Yamoussoukro, the "Grand Route," is a four-lane divided highway. Most of the other roads are finished with gravel and crushed stone or have been left as unimproved dirt roads. Few people in Ivory Coast own a car. Most Ivorians get around cities by taxi or bus and travel between villages and towns by "bush taxi." That could be an old car, a converted truck, or a bus. During the rainy season, the dirt roads are muddy ruts. In the dry season passengers and vehicles are covered with dust.

One of Ivory Coast's few paved roads goes through prosperous farmland and has telephone wires running along the side.

Ivory Coast's one railroad runs from Abidjan to Ouagadougou in Burkina Faso. It links Ivory Coast's northern cities and manufacturing plants to the port at Abidjan. Many industries have been built along the route.

Ivory Coast now has three airports with permanent surface runways. They include the international airport at Abidjan-Port Bouët and the airports at Yamoussoukro and Bouaké. Ivory Coast's other large towns have smaller airports, and there are about fifty private airfields throughout the country. Air Ivoire is Ivory Coast's national airline. It connects Ivory Coast cities to one another and to neighboring countries. Air Afrique, one of Africa's international airlines, was formed by ten former French colonies, including Ivory Coast. Air Afrique's headquarters is in Abidjan.

Few Ivorians own telephones, radios, or televisions. Those who do can choose from thirteen television stations and twenty radio stations. Ivorians frequently catch radio and television broadcasts while visiting friends, neighbors, or relatives who have sets. In addition, shortwave radios pick up broadcasts from neighboring countries, the Middle East, Europe, and the Voice of America.

One daily morning paper, *Fraternité Matin,* and two evening papers, *Ivoir' Soir* and *Bonsoir,* are published. Weekly publications include *Fraternité Hebdo, Ivoire Dimanche, Abidjan 7 Jours, Le Griot,* and *Le Guido.* All Ivorian publications are in French.

Above: Children in a Senufo village, with its round huts and raised maize-drying crib
Top right: A baby girl getting a bath
Right: A man wearing a pagne draped over a Western suit and a leopard-tooth headdress

Chapter 7

THE PEOPLE AND CULTURE OF CÔTE D'IVOIRE

In 1993 Ivory Coast's estimated population was 13,459,000. About 70 percent of the people belong to four major cultural groups: the Akan in the southeast, the Kru in the southwest, the Mandé in the northwest, and the Voltaic in the north-central and northeast. Within these four groups are sixty different ethnic groups.

Close to 30 percent of Ivory Coast's population is made up of foreigners. About one-half of them are farm laborers from Burkina Faso. Other African residents include unskilled workers from Guinea, Mali, and Ghana. Almost 200,000 Lebanese bankers and businesspeople form another large group. A French population of 30,000 remains in Ivory Coast. Business and government officials from the United States, Belgium, Switzerland, Spain, and other European countries also live here.

Ivory Coast is fast becoming an urban society. By 1990, 40 percent of the population lived in large towns and cities. More than one-half of the city dwellers live in and around Abidjan. The

Near the larger cities, villages of huts (right) are being replaced by modern suburban housing (above), with indoor plumbing and electricity.

rural population also is unevenly distributed. Most villagers live in the southeast, south-central, and north-central parts of the country. Smaller groups of villagers are clustered throughout the southwest, northwest, and northeast corners of Ivory Coast.

THE BAOULÉ

Ivory Coast's largest ethnic group is the Baoulé. They belong to the Akan cultural group. In the 1700s, the Baoulé fled what is now Ghana and settled between the Komoé and Bandama Rivers in central Ivory Coast. Their villages and cities are still in that region. Cities with large Baoulé populations include Bouaké and Yamoussoukro. In the villages, each family has a compound made up of rectangular houses facing a courtyard. Baoulé women live with their husbands' families, although Baoulés belong to their mothers' family groups rather than to their fathers' groups. In traditional Baoulé society today, power and land are passed on through a mother's family line to her sisters' sons. In that way, a man represents the family's line in the village council of elders.

Although many Baoulé have become Christians, they still

observe rituals that worship the spirits of ancestors. Each year during the harvest festival, the first yam is offered to the ancestors. Each Baoulé family line claims ownership of a ceremonial stool that represents the spirit of the founding ancestor of the mother's family. The family's male leader sits on this stool on important occasions. The Baoulé are famous for their small finely carved wooden statues that symbolize ancestral spirits.

Over two centuries, the Baoulé, as a group, achieved great power by absorbing smaller neighboring groups into their society. This occurred partly through warfare and intermarriage. Many Baoulé villages developed close ties through trade. By building a network of interconnected people, the Baoulé now dominate Ivorian politics. This ethnic group also gained a controlling interest in most areas of the economy. The Baoulé were one of the first Ivorian ethnic groups to become coffee and cocoa planters. Today many of the country's large plantations are owned by Baoulé, as are many factories and banks. Most Baoulé, however, are small farmers who grow coffee and cocoa as cash crops. To feed themselves, they raise yams, catch fish, and hunt wild game.

THE SENUFO

The Senufo, Ivory Coast's second-largest ethnic group, are part of the larger Voltaic cultural group. They live on the north-central savanna. Some cities with large Senufo populations are Korhogo, Katiola, and Ferkéssédougou. Senufo villages are divided into several quarters. Within each quarter, family compounds are arranged in a circle around a courtyard. The villages' streets wind in mazelike fashion among the compounds. Traditional Senufo

Left: *The thatched round house of a Senufo wife*
Above: *A Dyula weaver*

houses are made of mud and straw bricks with thatch roofs. Rather than rethatch a roof, some Senufo now install corrugated metal ones. The men live in rectangular houses; their wives, in round ones.

A special Senufo institution is called *poro*. Every seven years, a new group of boys from each quarter of a Senufo village forms a poro group. The boys pass through three stages of initiation, which are completed when they are in their thirties. At each stage, they learn more about Senufo social traditions, traditional religions, and farming practices. For example, they learn how to lead special ceremonies for harvests and funerals.

The instruction and initiations take place within a sacred grove of trees outside the village. A strong bond is formed among the members of each poro. Because many men now leave their villages for school or for city jobs, fewer men are able to complete the many years of poro.

All Senufo villagers are farmers. Their main cash crops are

These life-sized sculptures show the skill of Ivorian artists.

cotton, rice, and groundnuts (peanuts). They also grow rice, maize, millet, and vegetables for their own use. Maize is stored in round, mud-brick cribs. To keep out rodents and insects, the cribs are raised on clay legs. Senufo raise goats and chickens. They get beef and milk from Fulani cattle herders who set up camps outside Senufo villages.

During the off-season from farming, some Senufo pursue specialized crafts that are passed down from father to son and from mother to daughter. These Senufo are expert wood carvers and potters. Masks, drums, and doors carved by Senufo men are works of art. The masks and drums play important roles in Senufo poro ceremonies. Senufo women make clay pots of various sizes without a potter's wheel. Their reddish-orange pottery is sometimes flecked with brown or black bark during the cooling process.

In most Senufo families, land ownership and village power traditionally come through the mother's line to her sisters' sons. In other ethnic groups, it traditionally comes from the father's line. In both cases, actual control of land and power is held by men.

THE BÉTÉ

Ivory Coast's third-largest ethnic group is the Bété. They are part of the southwestern Kru language group. Bété villages are found in the rain forest between the cities of Daloa, Gagnoa, and Soubré. The Bété are members of their father's family line. When a Bété woman marries, her husband's family pays her family a "bride price." That money or another gift is meant to compensate the bride's family for losing her. It also makes legitimate any children of the marriage, because inheritances are passed down through the father.

The Bété resisted the French during colonial times and have openly disagreed with the Ivorian government since then. In 1970, Gnabé Opadjelé, a Bété leader, wanted to run for president of Ivory Coast. President Houphouët-Boigny would not allow that. When Opadjelé requested a place in the Council of Ministers and

Cattle play an important role in both the lives and the economy of the Malinké.

was turned down, he led government protesters to Gagnoa. On the way, he was captured by government troops, ending the rebellion.

Today the Bété are known as prosperous producers of coffee and cocoa beans. They also stand out because they have a large Christian community. Many Bété now live in cities, including Gagnoa, Daloa, and the coastal city of Abidjan.

THE MALINKÉ

The Malinké, Ivory Coast's fourth-largest ethnic group, are part of the northern Mandé cultural group. Their towns and villages stand in the northwestern Ivory Coast. Odienné is Ivory Coast's largest town in Malinké country. High fences surround many Malinké villages. Within the fences stand groups of round, mud brick homes with cone-shaped straw roofs.

Most of the Malinké follow the Muslim religion. Muslim Malinké traders are called Dyula. Their main crops are millet, cotton, and sorghum. Today most Malinké are farmers and cattle herders. The Malinké raise cattle as a sign of wealth as well as for food. The cattle also are used to pay the "bride price" before a Malinké marriage takes place. As with the Bété, power and possessions are passed down through Malinké fathers' families.

A dance being performed at an initiation ceremony for young Dan men

THE DAN

The Dan, a southern Mandé language group, live in the mountains and forests near Man and Danané in far western Ivory Coast. They raise rice and cassava on terraces built into hills and mountains. They grow rubber and coffee and gather kola nuts as cash crops. The Dan sell most of the nuts to traders from Mali. When Dan men are not farming, many of them work as lumberjacks in the timber industry. Others work on the docks or as domestic help in Ivory Coast's western cities.

The Dan are great artists and craftspeople. They paint murals on their round, mud-brick houses. First, a wide band of white clay is spread on the outside walls. Then designs from Dan history are

A Dan dancer in one of the people's famous black masks

drawn on the clay using red dyes. The Dan also have gained fame as carvers of masks. The best-known ones are carved almost paper-thin from hardwoods and then varnished to a glossy black sheen.

RELIGION

Religious beliefs and rituals play an important part in Ivorian daily life. Long before Christian missionaries arrived along the coast and Muslims appeared on the savanna, ethnic groups had developed their own religious practices. Today, about 60 percent of Ivorians observe local religions. Most of these people live in villages, although when Ivorians move to the cities, they take their local beliefs with them. More than 25 percent of Ivorians are Muslims, and about 12 percent are Christians.

In most traditional Ivorian religions, people must conduct themselves properly toward one another and toward their ancestors. Traditional practices sometimes honor the spirits of ancestors through offerings of food and drink. In that way, ancestors are asked to give good luck or to take away bad luck. Followers of

The spectacular St. Paul's Cathedral in Abidjan easily brings to mind Ivory Coast's most famous inhabitants, the elephants.

some traditional religions believe that living people also have spirits. These spirits determine each person's character and personality. Other traditional religions believe in gods that control the rain, the harvest, and other elements in nature.

Some traditional religions have priests. Others recognize that diviners have special powers. Ivorians seek help from diviners for many problems, including those caused by sorcery. Diviners use special clothes, powders, and statuettes to attract spirits. The spirits tell them what is causing illness, trouble between two people, or poor crops. The spirits also tell the diviners what the person must do to solve the problem, such as wear an amulet or sacrifice a chicken or goat.

A majority of Ivory Coast's Christians are Roman Catholic. Missions with churches, schools, and seminaries for training

The interior of the great dome of the Basilica of Our Lady of Peace in Yamoussoukro rises 525 feet (160 meters) above the ground. It was built by Félix Houphouët-Boigny and consecrated by Pope John Paul II in 1990.

priests are scattered across the country. Most Catholics, however, live in cities or villages in the southeast. Methodists, Baptists, and some evangelicals are other Christian groups. They also live in cities or in villages in the southeast.

Harrism is a uniquely Ivorian Christian religion. In 1914 William Wade Harris, a Liberian, started preaching along the coast. He called on Ivorians to lead a simple life, become Christians, and give up their amulets and traditional beliefs. Some of his followers became Catholics or Methodists. Today Harrism is practiced by about 100,000 Ivorians, mainly along the eastern coast.

The location and size of Ivory Coast's Muslim population has changed in recent years. Many Muslims have moved south from the savanna, hoping to find work in southern cities. Some southern city dwellers have converted to Islam. Muslims are supposed to observe five pious duties—make a profession of faith, pray five times each day, give to the poor, fast during the month of Ramadan, and make a pilgrimage to Mecca in Saudi Arabia, if they can afford it. Mecca was the birthplace of Muhammad, the founder of Islam. Many Ivorian Muslims strictly follow the five pious duties. Some well-to-do Ivorians take special airplane flights

Left: The Grand Mosque in Yamoussoukro
Above: A Muslim mosque in an outlying village

to Mecca. Some Ivorian Muslims continue to take part in ritual dances and hold beliefs from traditional religions. However, this is gradually decreasing through the work of Muslim teachers.

Towns and villages with large Muslim populations have one or more mosques. Older Ivorian mosques are tall, rounded, cone-shaped buildings made of mud bricks. Surrounding some of these mosques are shorter ornamental cones. As the mosques were built, large sticks were stuck into the sides. They serve as scaffolding when the mosques are replastered with mud. Newer mosques are made of concrete, and many of them look like mosques found in the Middle East.

FOOD AND CLOTHING

Ivorian food tends to be quite spicy. Rice with a peppery peanut sauce is a special dish on the northern savanna. Fish with fried plantains is served near the coast. The national dish is *foutou*, a sticky dough of mashed plantains or yams dipped by hand into

Left: Special to West Africa is the pagne, *a long piece of woven fabric worn by women in a variety of ways. It is very useful as a carrier for an infant. Above: Akan village women pounding the ingredients for* foutou

a spicy meat or fish sauce. Millet and maize form the basis of most meals. Groups of women gather in city and village courtyards to grind maize in large wooden mortars with long wooden pestles, which they also use to pound foutou. In good weather, they cook their family's meals in ceramic or metal pots outdoors on small stone hearths. In bad weather, they prepare the food indoors.

The best-known piece of Ivorian clothing is the pagne, worn by both men and women. Women wear it as a skirt or arrange it as a dress. For special occasions men sometimes drape a traditional pagne around themselves. Today, most pagne cloth is made in textile mills, but some pagne cloth is still handwoven.

LANGUAGES

Each of Ivory Coast's sixty ethnic groups has its own spoken language. Most Ivorians speak at least two languages. They speak their own ethnic language plus the Dyula language. Dyula is the language of trade. Ivorians use it when they go to the marketplace.

Educated Ivorians also converse in French and frequently English. Although French is the official language and is widely used in government, it is spoken only by Ivorians who have an elementary or high-school education. French is heard mainly in the cities.

STORYTELLERS AND WRITERS

Storytellers remain important people in Ivorian society, because almost one-half of the people cannot read or write. The storytellers orally pass on traditional poetry, folktales, and myths. Through these stories Ivorians learn about nature, their society's values, religion, and history. Among the Malinké in northwestern Ivory Coast, storytellers are sometimes called *griots.*

Ivorians who can read will find little that is written in any of their sixty ethnic languages. Books by most Ivorian writers are in French. They often deal with the problems that Ivorians face in being part of two very diverse cultures—French urban culture and their ethnic village group culture. Unfortunately, some educated Ivorians are ashamed of their rural backgrounds. Other Ivorians now realize that the richness of their village traditions soon will be lost if the educated few neglect to write about their ancient heritages.

Two of Ivory Coast's best-known writers are Bernard B. Dadié and Pierre Dupré. Besides writing poems, short stories, and novels, Dadié has served in many government posts, including minister of cultural affairs. In 1960 Dupré received the Literary Prize for Black African Expression in French for his novel *Kocoumbo, A Black Student.*

Clockwise from above: A cabinetmaker in the Tai region; the new Ivory Intercontinental Hotel with a massive "totem" pole of Ivorian carvings as its symbol; and a wood carver at work on a huge head.

ARTS AND CRAFTS

Ivorian artists, in contrast to the writers, use many ideas from Ivorian stories and beliefs as well as traditional materials. Youssouf Bath draws masks, sacred festivals, and hunters and wild animals on bark cloth and paper. Ouattara, a Senufo artist, attaches masks and objects used by diviners to his canvases. Gerard Santoni uses Baoulé designs and sometimes attaches Baoulé striped fabric to his works. Christian Lattier is famous for his sculptures made from iron covered with rope.

To become a wood sculptor takes many years of hard training. Many carvers still learn their skills from their fathers. Today, other artists receive training in art schools in Bingerville and Abidjan or in special art centers in other towns. Many Senufo and Baoulé artists make "tourist art," copies of traditional masks and small statues that Americans and Europeans buy to display in their homes. One Baoulé carver, Koffi Konakou, carves modern items such as baseball caps, dressy shoes, and computers.

Ivory Coast's traditional wooden sculptures are known around the world. Small gold and brass sculptures also are world famous. Some small sculptures include masks, statuettes, fly whisks, and canes used in religious or social ceremonies. Large traditional wooden sculptures such as drums, granary doors, and ceremonial stools are each made from one piece of wood. Some Ivorians believe that each sculpture takes on the life of the tree from which it is made. Sculptors or carvers must search for just the right tree. Before a tree can be cut down, the village chief, diviner, and carvers hold a special ceremony in which a sacrifice to the earth is made.

Masks are still used in traditional Ivorian ceremonies. Each mask has a different purpose. Some are meant to bring peace or a good harvest. Others ask for vengeance for wrongs done to a family or a village. Still others are used in funerals, for initiation ceremonies of the young, or just for entertainment. Masks can sit on top of the head, cover the face, or conceal the whole body. Body

Mask dancers and musicians performing at the international airport in Yamoussoukro

masks are made of cotton. Old masks are believed to have great powers. Because of these special powers, masks are kept hidden when not in use. Women and children are forbidden to look at some of the powerful masks.

To the Ivorians, a person does not just put on a mask but becomes the spirit of the mask. The mask acts as a link to the spirit world. The masks lead villagers in the ceremonies. They always are accompanied by singing and dancing.

MUSIC, DANCE, AND FESTIVALS

Music plays an important part in traditional religious events and in everyday activities such as fishing, hunting, and farming. Most singing is done by a group. Songs deal with nature, religion,

A balafon is an echoing musical instrument used by the people of the border area between Ivory Coast and Burkina Faso.

history, and everyday life. Traditional instruments include carved drums, whistles, fifes, horns, and flutes of ivory. One of the most interesting Ivorian instruments is the balafon—the Ivorian version of the xylophone. The balafon has wooden strips of different lengths placed over hollow gourds of various sizes. When the strips of wood are struck by rubber-tipped sticks, musical tones are produced.

Ivorians also enjoy modern music from Europe and America. The Abidjan Orchestral Ensemble performs classical music. As they walk through village streets, teenagers listen to rock music on transistor radios. European and American dances are sometimes performed during village festivals.

Traditional dances still play a part in ceremonies and festivals. They might tell a story about the history and beliefs of an ethnic group or simply serve as entertainment. During the Senufo N'Goron Dance, young girls move forward and backward lightly and quickly like chickens scratching the ground. They wave colorful fly whisks in each hand. On their backs, they wear a large tassel of straw plumes that looks like a bird's tail. On Sundays in

A choir of flutes made from the hollowed tusks of elephants

the Indénié Kingdom, dances are performed to the beat of sacred drums.

Independence Day in Ivory Coast is August 7, but it is not celebrated until December 7. In August the farmers still have about a month to wait before the harvest is ready and another month or more before they are paid. The people have little food and less money, so August is not a time for celebration. December is a time for feasting and dancing. Village women often buy matching pagnes and dance together.

Nature also dictates the Harmattan Winds Festival. Each January, a week-long, international hang-gliding festival is held at Zala. Gliders from all over the world leap off a 1,600-foot (488-meter) cliff and are lifted into the air by the harmattan winds.

The modern city of Abidjan, located on the Ébrié Lagoon

Chapter 8

A TOUR THROUGH CÔTE D'IVOIRE

Ivory Coast's cities stand in sharp contrast to its villages. Gleaming office buildings, condominiums, and French restaurants rise up in Abidjan. Traffic jams and an increasing crime rate mar that city's streets. Depending on the season, muddy or dusty roads lead to most Ivory Coast villages. Villagers live in homes much like those of their ancestors hundreds of years ago. Rural Ivorians farm their fields, make pottery, and perform tradition rituals.

ABIDJAN: PEARL OF THE LAGOONS

Abidjan is on Ébrié Lagoon, at the center of the southeastern lagoon region. One of the city's nicknames is "Pearl of the Lagoons." Another nickname is "First City." With more than 2.5 million people, Abidjan is Ivory Coast's largest city. It has become the economic, cultural, and tourist capital of the country. Until 1983 it was also the political capital. Much of the government's work continues to take place here, even though the capital was officially moved to Yamoussoukro.

Abidjan is laid out in five districts: the Plateau, Cocody,

Many apartments in Abidjan are located over stores in shopping districts (above). The large open market at Treichville, a district within Abidjan, is famous for its variety of foods (right).

Marcory, Treichville, and Adjame. They are separated from one another by bays and the lagoon. The Plateau District is the heart of Abidjan's business center. High-rise glass-and-steel office buildings mark the skyline. Bankers and businesspeople dine in French restaurants and shop in European-style stores and boutiques. Because of its high style, Abidjan has still another nickname, "Paris of Africa."

Americans, Europeans, and wealthy Ivorians live along the hedge-lined streets of the Cocody and Marcory Districts. Their homes are air-conditioned mansions with beautiful gardens and swimming pools. Many of these houses are surrounded by fences and gates and have security alarms. Government buildings and foreign embassies are located in Marcory. The futuristic St. Paul's Cathedral hugs Marcory's shore. The Hôtel Ivoire towers above the Cocody District. This hotel is almost a city in itself. Tourists and Ivorians alike use its shops, restaurants, bowling alleys, and wraparound swimming pool. The hotel's ice-skating rink is the only one in West Africa. Ivory Coast's only casino is in Cocody, but

Immigrant washermen in the Banco River do laundry for the better-off residents of Adjame (left). A large sports arena in Abidjan draws fans from all walks of life (right).

only foreign tourists may gamble here.

More than two-thirds of Abidjan's population live in the over-crowded Treichville and Adjame Districts. Half of these residents are Ivorians; the other half are from other West African countries. Ivory Coast's ethnic groups have set up separate communities within Treichville and Adjame. In that way, each group can continue to practice its traditional customs. Ethnic restaurants serve foods special to each group. In Adjame, the Banco laundry-men, mostly immigrant workers from Burkina Faso, wash clothes by beating them on the rocks in the Banco River. They do not make laundry marks on the clothes or give their customers receipts. Yet, it is rare that they lose an order.

Treichville is famous for its open-air market. In separate stalls, vendors sell everything from traditional handmade cloth to plastic

The narrow barrier island at Assini, site of the first French settlement in the Ivory Coast, is now a luxurious Club Méditerranée Resort that draws visitors from all over. The water to the left is one of the many lagoons in this region of Ivory Coast.

buckets. Food vendors, called *maquis*, hawk fresh pineapples and exotic, spicy dishes. Shoppers are expected to bargain for their purchases. Vendors enjoy customers who drive a hard bargain. In other stalls, *juju* doctors make *gris-gris*, or good luck charms, from the fur, hide, and teeth of wild animals. At night, Treichville becomes even more lively as the sounds of African music fill the air. Ivorians dance to its beat on the cobblestone streets.

Abidjan is known for its cultural attractions. The National Museum displays Ivorian art, masks, jewelry, and sculpture. The National University of Ivory Coast, in Cocody, draws students from around the country, as well as from other West African states. Theater productions of African dramas and folklore are performed at the Treichville Cultural Center and Cocody's City Theater.

Just north of Abidjan is Banco National Park. Its 7,000 acres (2,835 hectares) lie along the Banco River. Families enjoy walking and picnicking in the tropical forest. Some also visit the park's zoo.

OTHER CITIES IN THE LAGOON REGION

Assini is near the southeastern tip of Ivory Coast. This village is about 50 miles (80 kilometers) from Abidjan on the Aby Lagoon. Assini was the first site chosen for French settlement in 1687. Ivory Coast's first French school and first coffee plantation also were established at Assini. Today, vacationers play or relax on the white sand beaches. They can take a break and eat some fresh coconut from the village's coconut groves. Adults enjoy privacy at Assini's Club Méditerranée Resort.

About 27 miles (44 kilometers) east of Abidjan is Grand-Bassam. This Ébrié Lagoon city served as the first French colonial capital of Ivory Coast from 1843 to 1900. Ivorians in Grand-Bassam keep both their colonial and ethnic histories alive. In the Old Quarter, the Governor's Palace has been restored. It now houses a collection of traditional ethnic clothing. In the 1980s, the government established an artisan's village in Grand-Bassam. Here, people from Ivory Coast's ethnic groups explain how their crafts are made. In November each year, the N'Zima ethnic group holds its colorful Abissa festival.

Across the narrow Ébrié Lagoon from Grand-Bassam is Bingerville. It is

Girls in traditional dress prepare for a wedding at Grand Bassam.

surrounded by cocoa and coffee plantations. Bingerville served as Ivory Coast's second French colonial capital from 1900 to 1934. A reminder of the city's colonial past is the Governor's Mansion, which is now an orphanage. At the Bingerville School of Art, artists learn to blend European and traditional Ivorian designs.

West of Abidjan, on the Tadio Lagoon, are the towns of Grand Lahou, Gomon, and Tiagba. Grand-Lahou has a bustling business area and beautiful beaches. Gomon is home to the Abidji ethnic group's Dipri festival. Visitors who want to watch these rituals must arrive the night before. On that night, all the village's gates are locked. The next day participants in the ritual go into a mass frenzy. They are believed to be possessed by spirits. Some dancers plunge knives into their own bodies. Medicine men heal their wounds with salves of kaolin (clay), herbs, and raw eggs. To the southwest is the fishing village of Tiagba. All the buildings rest on stilts at the edge of the lagoon.

CENTRAL IVORY COAST

A great highway links Abidjan to Yamoussoukro, called the "Radiant City." It was once a small Baoulé village in the rain forest. Yamoussoukro was the birthplace of Félix Houphouët-Boigny. After he became president of Ivory Coast, he transformed Yamoussoukro into a showplace for modern architecture. The city has been Ivory Coast's official capital since 1983. Today, its large hotels and government buildings stand along broad, palm-lined boulevards. Many of them are half empty because most government offices have remained in Abidjan.

A high wall surrounds the Presidential Palace. On the palace

When the Roman Catholic "Basilica in the Bush" built by Félix Houphouët-Boigny was consecrated, people came to Yamoussoukro from all over the world. Many local women wore pagne designs advertising Ivory Coast.

grounds are the huts and sacred meeting tree of the old village. Village chiefs held palaver under the tree. They listened to villagers' requests and complaints and then issued decisions.

Monuments of the Catholic and Muslim religions are found in Yamoussoukro. The Basilica of Our Lady of Peace is the largest church in Africa. Some call it the "Basilica in the Bush." Houphouët-Boigny had the special church built on his land with his family's money. Estimates place the total building expenses at close to $300 million. After Pope John Paul II consecrated the church in 1990, Houphouët-Boigny gave it to the Vatican. The basilica's dome is 380 feet (116 meters) high and, combined with the rest of the building, it reaches 525 feet (160 meters) above the ground. It is supported by sixty columns. Thirty-six huge stained-glass windows take up most of the wall space. The basilica seats 7,000 people and has standing room for more than 10,000 in the

Left: The Harmattan Hotel at Bouaké
Right: At nearby Katiola, Mongoro potters sell their beautiful pots.

plaza. Because Ivory Coast has few Catholics, the basilica gets little use. It was filled to capacity, however, for Houphouët-Boigny's funeral.

Nearby stands a mosque built in North African style. Its rectangular walls are decorated with shiny mosaic tiles. Although much smaller than the basilica, it serves many prayerful Muslims several times a day.

Northwest of Yamoussoukro, Kossou Lake covers 650 square miles (1,684 square kilometers). This artificially made lake on the Bandama River has been stocked with fish. Fishermen from Mali have built villages along the lake. They sell their catches from the lake in nearby markets. West of the lake is Marahoué National Park, with many kinds of butterflies in its forests. White-collared mangabey monkeys and mona monkeys live in the trees.

North of Yamoussoukro, almost in the exact middle of Ivory

Coast, is Bouaké, Ivory Coast's second-largest city. Each March, a week-long carnival is held there. Bouaké is the industrial and transportation center of the country's interior. The Gonfreville Mills is the nation's oldest and largest textile factory. Chemicals, cigarettes, packaged food, and soap are made in other Bouaké factories. Several highways and Ivory Coast's only railroad run through the city. Most Ivory Coast television shows are broadcast from Bouaké. The television complex offers tours to the public. In the midst of these examples of modern technology, a traditional native market thrives.

THE SOUTHWESTERN FOREST FRONTIER

San Pédro is in the center of the southwestern coast. Like most coastal cities, San Pédro started as a fishing village. In recent years, it has become the country's newest modern city. More than fifty thousand people live here. San Pédro's location in the rain forest has made it a logging center. Timber and paper-processing factories are among its biggest businesses. San Pédro also has beautiful sandy beaches that attract tourists from

Tai National Park, near San Pédro, is Africa's only remaining rain forest.

A small fishing boat on the beach near Sassandra

around the world. Many of them come to catch record-breaking blue marlin. In 1990 a group of Americans on the *Yamoussoukro* caught the world's heaviest blue marlin up to that time.

East of San Pédro lies Sassandra, once Ivory Coast's largest port city. It has now been rebuilt as a vacation center. Tourists can stay at new hotels and enjoy campsites on the beach. West of San Pédro is Tabou, home of the Kru people.

THE MOUNTAINS OF MAN

Man is the largest city in the western Ivory Coast. Surrounded by mountains, it is called the "Town with Eighteen Peaks." Mountain climbers use the city as a base, and local villagers serve as guides. Mount Dent is not the highest mountain in the area, but it is one of the most interesting. Ivorians call this mountain "The Sacred Guardian" or "Guardian Angel." Its rugged, toothlike shape beckons many climbers. On the way to the top, they must

Above: The only way to cross this river near Odienné is by a precarious bridge.
Right: Visitors to Gouéssésso can study Ivorian folklore firsthand when dancers wear Dan masks.

overcome huge rocks, deep crevices, and mamba snakes.

The Mountains of Toura and Mounts Tonkou and Kahoué are a few of the higher mountains. Ivory Coast's highest peak, Mount Nimba, can now be reached directly by highway from Man. As in the past, Man is still an important trading center. Its huge, two-story market overflows with food and crafts. In the crafts district, ivory carvers make jewelry and statues and leather workers braid strips of leather into necklaces.

Man is also the center of the Dan people's homeland. At nearby Gouéssésso, a hotel has been built to look like a Dan village. Villagers there demonstrate traditional weaving and pottery making. In other towns and villages, the Dan perform ancient dances using traditional masks. Touba is famous for the stilt dance, in which masked dancers on 10-foot (3-meter)-high stilts do somersaults and other acrobatic tricks. In other villages, young girls covered with jewelry are juggled by men holding daggers.

Left: A country road near Fakaha
Right: Komoé National Park is a major wildlife sanctuary near Korhogo.

VILLAGES AND CITIES OF THE SAVANNA

Korhogo, with a population of more than forty-five thousand, is the largest city on Ivory Coast's savanna. It is also in the middle of Senufo country and serves as a center of Senufo culture. The Gbon Coulibaly Museum displays traditional carved Senufo masks known for their huge size. Senufo dancers led by a masked dancer perform the Panther Dance in Korhogo. At Korhogo's Center of Artisans, Senufo potters, sculptors, blacksmiths, and weavers display their ancient skills. In the main market, shoppers can buy masks and statues carved especially for the tourist trade. Brass bracelets, carved wooden boxes, and hand-painted linen are available. Many Muslims also live in Korhogo. Their mosque rises from the town's hill.

Some nearby villages are known for special crafts. In Waraniene, Dyula weavers use handcrafted looms to make sturdy cotton cloth. Artists in Fakaha paint designs onto lengths of raw linen. They use black, brown, and orange dyes from bark and

Earth-tone paintings on cotton cloth are created by Fakaha artists.

vegetables. Kani's blacksmiths produce dabas, the Senufo's main farm tool.

In Boundiali, west of Korhogo, good examples of traditional Senufo architecture can be seen. Houses, both rectangular and round, are made of mud with straw-thatch roofs. Circular granaries with cone-shaped thatch roofs stand on clay legs. Young girls, accompanied by tom-toms, flutes, and balafons, perform the N'Goron Dance.

The Muslim towns of Ferkéssédougou and Kong are east of Korhogo. Ferkéssédougou is an economic center of northern Ivory Coast. In recent years, sugarcane and rice plantations were begun here. The northernmost Ivorian stop on the Ivory Coast-Burkina Faso railroad is in Ferkéssédougou. Kong is a great center of Muslim culture. Beautiful mosques from the seventeenth century have been rebuilt here.

At the southernmost point of the eastern savanna, close to the Ghana border, stands Bondoukou. It is one of Ivory Coast's oldest cities. Just west of town, visitors stop to study ancient tombs that are decorated with sculptures. Today, Bondoukou is the center of the Abron kingdom.

LOOKING TO THE FUTURE

From modern Abidjan to ancient Bondoukou, Ivory Coast presents a mosaic of many people, religions, and cultures living

Abidjan at night, a sparkling "gem" in the "Jewel of West Africa"

together in peace. Life goes on in Ivorian villages much as it has for hundreds of years. Villagers practice their traditional crafts, customs, and beliefs. These villagers, however, are willing to plant new crops and try better ways of growing old ones. At the same time, thousands of Ivorians have moved to the country's large cities. There, the lucky ones go to school or find jobs in Ivory Coast's new factories.

By learning from the past while moving into the future, Ivory Coast has become the richest country in West Africa. Even though Ivorians have experienced a drop in income in recent years, they still live better than most other Africans. However, Ivorian leaders must work at narrowing the gap between its many poor villagers and the few wealthy business owners. They must also continue to create opportunities for more people to take part in government. If Ivory Coast's leaders can accomplish these tasks, the country will remain the "Jewel of West Africa," and the Ivorian miracle will continue as an example for all nations of the world.

Abengourou	C3			
Abidjan	D3			
Aboisso	D4			
Aby (lagoon)	D4			
Adiaké	D4			
Adzopé	C4			
Afféry	C4			
Agboville	D3			
Agmbilékrou	C4			
Akoupé	C4			
Ananda	C3			
Anyama	D3			
Arrah	C4			
Ayamé	D4			
Bagoé (river)	A2			
Bako	B2			
Bandama (river)	C3			
Bandama Rouge	B2			
Bangolo	C2			
Béoumi	C3			
Biankouma	C2			
Bin-Houyé	C1			
Bocanda	C3			
Bondoukou	B4			
Bongouanou	C3			
Borotou	B2			
Botro	C3			
Bouaflé	C3			
Bouaké	C3			
Bouandougou	B3			
Bouna	B4			
Boundiali	B2			
Brobo	C3			
Buyo	C2			
Cavally (river)	C1,D2			
Dabakala	B3			
Dabou	D3			
Daloa	C2			
Danané	C1			
Daoukro	C4			
Davo (river)	D3			
Diabo	C3	Kani	B2	
Dianra	B2	Katiola	B3	
Diawala	A3	Kokolopozo	D2	
Dikodougou	B3	Kolia	B2	
Dimbokro	C3	Komoé (river)	B4	
Divo	D3	Komoé National Park	B4	
Duékoué	C2	Konan	B1	
Ébrié (lagoon)	D3	Kong	B3	
Ferkéssédougou	B3	Korhogo	B3	
Fresco	D3	Koro	B2	
Gagnoa	C3	Kossou (lake)	C3	
Gbon	B2	Kotouba	B4	
Gonitafla	C3	Kouassi-Datékro	C4	
Goulia	A2	Koun-Fao	C4	
Grabo	D2	Kouto	B2	
Grand-Bassam	D4	Lakota	D3	
Grand-Lahou	D3	Leraba (river)	B3	
Gregbe	C2	Lobo (river)	C2	
Growa Point	D2	Logoualé	C2	
Guéyo	D2	M'bahiakro	C3	
Guibéroua	C2	M'batto	C3	
Guiglo	C2	M'bengué	B3	
Guitry	D3	Madinani	B2	
Half Assini	D4	Maminiqui	C3	
Issia	C2	Manignan	B2	
Jacqueville	D3	Mankono	B3	

Marahoué Nat'l Park	C2	Séquélon	B2	
Mount Kahoué	C2	Sianhala	A2	
Mount Kopé	D2	Sifié	C2	
Mount Niénokoué	D2	Sikensi	D3	
Mount Nimba	C1	Sinfra	C3	
Mount Peko Nat'l Park	C2	Sirasso	B2	
Mount Tonkou	C2	Soubré	D2	
Napiéolédougou	B3	Souroukaha	B3	
Nassian	B4	Tabou	D2	
Niellé	A3	Tadio (lagoon)	D3	
Nzi (river)	B3,C3	Tafiré	B3	
Nzo (river)	C2	Tanda	C4	
Odienné	B2	Téhini	B4	
Ouangolodougou	B3	Teogréla	A2	
Ouaninou	B2	Tiassalé	D3	
Ouellé	C3	Tiébissou	C3	
Oumé	C3	Tiémé	B2	
Ouragahio	C3	Tienigboué	B3	
Pakouabo	C3	Tienko	A2	
Port-Bouët	D3	Tioroniaradougou	B3	
Prikro	C4	Touba	B2	
Rubino	C3	Touléplu	C1	
Sakassou	C3	Toumodi	C3	
Sandama Blanc	B3	Toura Mountains	C2	
Sassandra	D2	Vavoua	C2	
Sassandra (river)	B2,D2	Yamoussoukro	C3	
Séquéla	C2	Zouan-Hounien	C1	
		Zuénoula	C2	

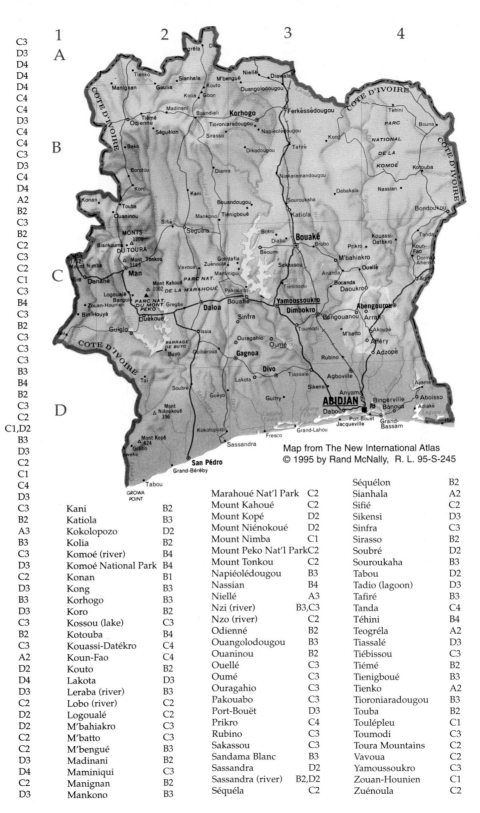

Map from The New International Atlas
© 1995 by Rand McNally, R. L. 95-S-245

MINI-FACTS AT A GLANCE

GENERAL INFORMATION

Official Name: *République de Côte d'Ivoire* (Republic of Ivory Coast)

Capital: Abidjan (legislative); Yamoussoukro (administrative)

Government: The government is a multiparty republic with one legislative house, the National Assembly. The president is the chief of state and the prime minister is the chief of government. Directly elected by the people for a five-year term, the president's powers include appointment and removal of ministers, judges, and military leaders. A Council of Ministers and the Economic and Social Council help the president in making administrative decisions. The judicial branch is made up of lower and superior courts. For administrative purposes, the country is divided into 49 prefectures and 129 municipalities.

Religion: The constitution guarantees freedom of religion to all citizens. About 60 percent of Ivorians observe traditional religions, 25 percent follow Islam, 12 percent are Christians (mostly Roman Catholics), and only 3 percent follow other religions. Many Ivorians who have converted to Christianity still observe rituals that worship the spirits of the ancestors. Harrism is a uniquely Ivorian Christian religion that preaches a simple lifestyle; some 100,000 Ivorians practice Harrism.

Ethnic Composition: Four major cultural groups are the Akan, the Kru, the Mandé, and the Voltaic; within these four groups are approximately sixty different ethnic groups. The Baoulé make up the largest ethnic group (some 20 percent of the population), followed by the Senufo, Bété, and Malinké. Close to 30 percent of the population is composed of foreigners from Burkina Faso, Guinea, Mali, Ghana, Lebanon, France, the United States, and Belgium.

Language: French is the official language, but it is spoken mainly by people with some education. Each of the sixty ethnic groups has its own spoken language. Most Ivorians speak their ethnic language plus Dyula, the language of trade.

National Flag: A vertical tricolor of orange, white, and green

National Emblem: A shield displaying an elephant's head in profile, flanked by two palm trees, with the rising sun above and a scroll bearing the legend *"République de Côte d'Ivoire"* beneath

National Anthem: *"L'Abidjanaise"* ("Greetings, O Land of Hope")

National Calendar: Gregorian

Money: The national currency is the Communauté Financière Africaine franc (CFA franc) of 100 centimes. In 1995 one CFA franc was worth $0.0020 in U.S. currency.

Membership in International Organizations: African Development Bank (ADB); Council of Entente; Economic Community of West African States (ECOWAS); International Cocoa Organization (ICCO); Nonaligned Movement; Organization of African Unity (OAU); West African Economic Community (CEAO)

Weights and Measures: Metric system

Population: 13,459,000 (1993 estimate); population density is 108 persons per sq. mi. (42 persons per sq km). About 40 percent of the people live in urban centers; 60 percent live in rural communities.

Cities:	
Abidjan	2,500,000
Bouaké	333,000
Daloa	123,000
Yamoussoukro	110,000
Gagnoa	85,000

(Populations based on 1988 estimates except Abidjan, which is 1990 estimate.)

GEOGRAPHY

Border: Ivory Coast's international border of 1,886 mi. (3,035 km) is shared by Liberia and Guinea in the west, Mali and Burkina Faso (formerly Upper Volta) in the north, and Ghana in the east. The Gulf of Guinea coastline is the southern boundary.

Coastline: 315 mi. (507 km) along the Gulf of Guinea

Land: Roughly square in shape, Ivory Coast is a vast plateau tilted toward the Atlantic Ocean in the south. The country can be divided into three regions. A narrow coastal belt, the lagoon region, is in the southeast along the Gulf of Guinea. It is fringed by sandy islands. The lagoons are linked to one another by small canals. The rain forest region is in the southwest and east central and covers about one-third of the country. The savanna region in the north provides grazing for the country's few cattle and produces most of the cotton. The only mountains are the eastern slopes of the Guinea Highlands along the Guinea border in the northwest. The coastline is generally smooth.

Highest Point: Mount Nimba at 5,748 ft. (1,752 m)

Lowest Point: Sea level

Rivers: The major rivers are the Cavally, Sassandra, Bandama, and Komoé—all running north to south into the Gulf of Guinea. Most are only seasonally navigable for a short distance—about 40 mi.; 64 km—because of rapids and waterfalls. Kossou Lake in the central part of the country is formed by a dam on the Bandama River. Lake Taabo is also a lake formed behind a hydroelectric dam.

Forests: Some four-fifths of the total land area is forest. True rain forests are in the south; they give way to scattered stands of deciduous trees in the north. Oil palms and coconut trees flourish along the coast. The major trees are mahogany, iroko (African teak), sipo, sau, avodire, and niangon. Excessive cutting and clearing of land to plant cash crops and to build roads are the main reason for excessive deforestation. The government runs a massive reforestation program.

Wildlife: Wildlife includes antelope, wild hogs, gazelles, kob antelopes, lions, crocodiles, elephants, hippopotamuses, cobras, green mambas, and pythons. Birds in the region include bush fowl, quail, partridges, bulbuls, hornbills, ducks, plovers, herons, egrets, and terns. The varied insect population includes deadly tsetse flies, mosquitoes, and termites. The Komoé National Park in the northeast is the largest (4,500 sq. mi.; 11,655 sq km) animal reserve. The Tai National Park in the southwest with pygmy hippopotamuses, chimpanzees, and antelopes is the only primary rain forest left in Africa. The Mount Nimba Reserve protects forest buffaloes, antelopes, bushbucks, and tree hyraxes.

Climate: Located just north of the equator, Ivory Coast's climate is marked by year-round high temperatures. In general, November is the hottest month and July is the coldest. There are two seasons—rainy and dry. The annual temperatures vary from 57° F (14° C) to 103° F (39° C). The highest annual rainfall—78 in.; 198 cm—is along the coast and in the southwest. The southern part of the country falls into the tropical zone, with hot and humid weather and heavy rains; daily temperatures vary from 72° F (22° C) to 91°F (32° C). The climate gets drier and hotter toward the north. The *harmattan* is the annual cold, dry northeasterly wind that blows down from the Sahara desert in December and January.

Greatest Distance: North to South: 420 mi. (676 km)

East to West: 411 mi. (661 km)

Area: 124,503 sq. mi. (322,463 sq km)

ECONOMY AND INDUSTRY

Agriculture: About 60 percent of the population is engaged in agricultural activities, and roughly half of the land is available for farming. Commercial crops are cocoa, coffee, rubber, pineapple, bananas, palm oil fruit, coconuts, cotton, and sugarcane; food crops are yams, plantains, cassava, taro, rice, maize, sorghum, millet, beans, and other vegetables. The country leads the world in cocoa bean production and is one of the major producers of coffee beans. Traditional methods of agriculture are used widely; tractors and threshers are used only on some large plantations and most farmers use a long cutting knife to clear the fields and a hoe to till the soil.

Fishing: Barracuda, carp, cavally, mackerel, marlin, mullet, sardines, shark, tarpon, tuna, shrimp, and crabs are common catches from the rivers, lagoons, and ocean. Most fish is eaten fresh; some is dried or smoked for export.

Mining: There are small deposits of bauxite, cobalt, copper, diamonds, manganese, and nickel. Gold and iron ores are of low grade. Two oil fields are offshore in the Gulf of Guinea; they were closed for oil production in the mid-1980s. Large natural gas fields exist near the oil fields. Electrical energy is derived from both thermal and hydroelectric plants.

Manufacturing: Small manufacturing factories produce food and wood products, cloth, chemicals, cement, lumber, furniture, plywood, and corrugated-steel roofing. Heavy industries produce air conditioners, freezers, refrigerators, paint, varnish, railroad cars, and heavy metals. There is an oil refinery at Vridi.

Transportation: In the early 1990s, there were 410 mi. (660 km) of railroad track, and 42,250 mi. (68,000 km) of roads, of which less than 10 percent are paved. During the rainy season, the dirt roads become muddy and difficult to travel. Abidjan is the busiest and finest seaport in western Africa; San Pédro is the country's second-largest seaport. With the construction of the Vridi Canal, oceangoing vessels are able to dock at the port of Abidjan. There are three airports with permanent surface runways and many smaller airports and airfields. Air Ivoire is the country's national airline. Abidjan is also the headquarters of Air Afrique, the airline of ten former French colonies.

Communication: Radio broadcasts are in French, English, and indigenous languages, but television is in French only. In the early 1990s, there was one radio receiver per 8 persons, one television set per 16 persons, and one telephone per 143 persons. Three daily newspapers—*Fraternité Matin, Ivoir' Soir,* and *Bonsoir*—are published.

Trade: The chief imports are crude and refined petroleum, machinery, transport equipment, food products, pharmaceuticals, plastics, paper and paper products, iron ore, chemicals, wheat flour, beef, fish, and milk. The major import sources are France, Nigeria, Japan, Germany, and the Netherlands. The chief export items are cocoa beans, coffee, fish, petroleum products, wood products, cotton, and cloth. The major customers are France, the Netherlands, Germany, Italy, Burkina Faso, Mali, Nigeria, Belgium, Luxembourg, and the United States.

EVERYDAY LIFE

Health: The major diseases are malaria, yellow fever, tetanus, polio, dysentery, yaws, pneumonia, measles, hookworm, and leprosy. Rural areas suffer from lack of running water and safe ways of waste disposal. In the early 1980s, there were almost 18,000 people per physician and one hospital bed per 800 persons. Private hospitals and clinics are encouraged by the government. Life expectancy at 53 years for males and 57 years for females is low compared to other nations. Infant mortality rate at 87 per 1,000 is high.

Education: Education is free at all levels and is conducted in French. There are three levels of public education: primary (six years), secondary (seven years), and higher. Many schools are overcrowded. There are several Catholic schools for both boys and girls and Qur'anic schools for boys only. The University of Ivory Coast at Abidjan, with about 20,000 students, is the country's major university. Many students attend colleges and universities in other countries. In the early 1990s the literacy rate was about 54 percent for men.

Holidays: New Year's Day, January 1
Labor Day, May 1
Independence Day, August 7 (celebrated on December 7)
All Saints' Day, November 1
Christmas, December 25

Movable religious holidays, which vary from year to year based on the Islamic lunar calendar, include *Id al-Fitr* and *Id al-Adha,* and Christian holidays based on the Gregorian calendar include Ascension Day and Whit Monday.

Culture: The country's traditional wooden, gold, and brass sculptures of masks, statuettes, fly whisks, canes, drums, and ceremonial stools are known around the world. Senufo women make clay pots of various sizes without a potter's wheel. The National Museum at Abidjan displays Ivorian art, masks, jewelry, and sculpture. The Gbon Coulibaly Museum displays oversized, traditional carved Senufo masks. The Basilica of Our Lady of Peace at Yamoussoukro is the largest church in Africa and one of the largest in the world.

Society: Both Baoulé and Senufo people belong to their mother's family group; power and land are passed down through a mother's family line to her sisters' sons. In the Bété group, inheritance is passed down through the father. *Poro* is a Senufo social institution in which every seven years a new group of boys pass through three stages of initiation that are completed when they are in their thirties. Praise singers, sometimes called *griots*, remain important in Ivorian society.

Dress: The *pagne* is the best-known Ivorian clothing worn mostly by women. It used to be woven by hand, but today most pagne cloth is made in textile mills. Western-style clothing is popular in urban areas.

Housing: Village families live in compounds of huts. Baoulé families live in rectangular houses while Senufo family compounds are arranged in a circle around a courtyard. High fences surround many Malinké villages of round mud-brick homes with cone-shaped straw roofs. The Dan people paint murals with white and red clay on their round, mud-brick houses. Traditional village houses are made of mud and straw bricks with thatch roofs or corrugated metal roofs. Circular granaries with cone-shaped thatch roofs stand on clay legs.

Food: The food is hot and spicy. Millet, maize, rice, yams, and cassava form the basis of most meals. Foutou, a dough of mashed yams or plantains dipped in a spicy meat or fish sauce, is the national dish. Other dishes are fish with fried plantains or with *affieke*, fermented cassava, and rice with a peppery peanut sauce.

Sports and Recreation: Soccer is popular. Music is important for traditional religious ceremonies and activities such as fishing, hunting, and farming. Traditional instruments include carved drums, whistles, fifes, and horns. The *balafon*, an Ivorian xylophone, is one of the most interesting Ivorian instruments. Teenagers listen to rock and roll via transistor radios. Traditional dances are part of ceremonies and festivals. The Harmattan Winds Festival is celebrated in January.

Social Welfare: Social security benefits provide compensation, retirement benefits, and allowances to wage-earning families. There is a minimum wage for workers in industry and commerce. The majority of the social welfare efforts are coordinated by religious and private organizations.

IMPORTANT DATES

8000 to 4000 B.C.—The earliest people live in present-day Ivory Coast

1500 B.C.—People make burial mounds of shells and broken pottery.

A.D. 200—Researchers believe about 250,000 people dwell in the area.

400–1600—Empires of Ghana, Mali, and Songhai rise and fall on the savannas; trade routes for gold and slaves cross the area.

622—The Prophet Muhammad establishes the religion of Islam in present-day Saudi Arabia.

1469—Portuguese explorer Soerio da Costa lands at Sassandra.

1637—A Catholic mission is established at Assini.

1687—The first French settlement is built at Assini.

1842–43—The first French forts are built at Assini and Grand-Bassam; palm oil is produced for the first time in large quantity.

1886—French government begins efforts to bring all of the Ivory Coast under its control.

1893—France officially proclaims Ivory Coast a French colony.

1895—Ivory Coast becomes part of French West Africa.

1898—Samory Touré is defeated and captured, leaving France in control of the north.

1899—A yellow fever epidemic spreads through Grand-Bassam.

1900—Bingerville becomes Ivory Coast's second French colonial capital.

1904—Ivory Coast becomes a constituent unit of the Federation of French West Africa (until 1958).

1914—William Wade Harris starts preaching a form of Christianity that later became known as *Harrism*.

1916—All of present-day Ivory Coast becomes a French colony.

1932—Some of the French colony of Upper Volta (now Burkina Faso) becomes part of Ivory Coast.

1934—Abidjan becomes Ivory Coast's new capital.

1936—The newly elected socialist government in France raises the minimum wage for Ivorians and passes other reforms; work begins on the Vridi Canal.

1944—The Brazzaville Conference results in far-reaching French government reforms that take place in 1946.

1945—*Syndicat Agricole Africain*, "African Agricultural Union" membership reaches 20,000; first election is held; Félix Houphouët-Boigny is elected to the French Constituent Assembly in Paris.

1946—Félix Houphouët-Boigny returns to Ivory Coast; he forms the *Parti Démocratique de la Côte d'Ivoire* (PDCI) and the *Rassemblement Démocratique Africain* (RDA).

1947—France separates the two colonies of Upper Volta and Ivory Coast.

1950—Work on the Vridi Canal is done, opening Abidjan to oceangoing ships.

1956—The French government passes more reforms for the people of Ivory Coast; all adults receive the right to vote.

1958—Ivory Coast votes to become a self-governing republic in the French Community.

1959—The country's first dam and hydroelectric plant are built on the Bia River; the Agni people attempt to break away from Ivory Coast and form an independent kingdom; national elections are held; Burkina Faso, Niger, Benin, and Ivory Coast form the Council of Entente.

1960—Ivory Coast becomes independent and withdraws from the French Community; a new constitution is adopted.

1961—An agreement is signed with France that will provide extensive military and economic aid.

1963—The University of Abidjan is founded; the Central Library in Abidjan-Treichville is founded.

1964—The country's second dam is built; several social customs such as polygamy, bride price, and matrilineal inheritance are abolished by law, but continue to be practiced by some Ivorians.

1968—The National Library is created in Abidjan.

1969—The Agni people again try to break away from Ivory Coast and form an independent kingdom; diplomatic relations with the Soviet Union are broken.

1972—A dam and hydroelectric plant are completed over the Bandama River; San Pédro, the second deep-water port, is opened.

1973—Ivory Coast breaks diplomatic relations with Israel; an agreement with France is renegotiated.

1974—A law prohibiting shooting of any wild animal in the Komoé National Park is passed; the prime minister of South Africa visits Ivory Coast.

1977—Petroleum is discovered.

1983—The process of transferring the national capital from Abidjan to Yamoussoukro (President Félix Houphouët-Boigny's birthplace) begins.

1985—President Félix Houphouët-Boigny helps negotiate peace between Mali and Burkina Faso over a border disagreement; national elections are held; the post of vice-president of the republic is abolished.

1986—The government requests that the French name—*Côte d'Ivoire*—be utilized as the official version in all languages.

1989—Work on *Nôtre Dame de la Paix* (Our Lady of Peace) Basilica is completed at the cost of $300 million; it is the largest Christian church in Africa and one of the largest in the world.

1990—Several strikes and student demonstrations are held to end one-party rule; multiparty elections are held for the first time; Pope John Paul II consecrates the Basilica of Our Lady of Peace.

l991—President Houphouët-Boigny hosts a peace conference in Yamoussoukro.

1993—Borders with Liberia reopened; President Félix Houphouët-Boigny dies.

1994—The CFA franc is devalued; three agreements are signed to develop the offshore oil and natural gas fields.

1995—Konan Bédié is elected president with more than 90 percent of the vote.

IMPORTANT PEOPLE

Aniaba, an African prince; educated and baptized as a Catholic at the court of King Louis XIV in France, he returned to Assini in 1701 and established a Catholic mission

Youssouf Bath, contemporary artist; draws masks, sacred pictures of hunters and wild animals on bark cloth and paper

Louis-Gustave Binger (1856–1936), French explorer and administrator; explored (1887-1889) south to Kong and made treaties with local chiefs to obtain land for French forts and posts; became governor of Ivory Coast in 1893

Soerio da Costa, Portuguese explorer; first European to land near Sassandra

Bernard Binlin Dadié (1916–), poet, short-story writer, and novelist; served in many government positions including minister of cultural affairs (1977)

Daniel Kablan Duncan, prime minister in 1993

Pierre Dupré (1927-   ), writer; writes in French; received the 1960 Literary Prize for Black African Expression in French for his novel *Kocoumbo, A Black Student*

Laurent Gbagbo (1945–), historian and leading figure of the political opposition; in exile in France until 1988, leads the *Front Populaire Invoirien* (FPI)

William Wade Harris (c. 1865-1929), a Liberian national; started Harrism, a Christian sect that preaches a simple lifestyle and giving up traditional beliefs

Dr. Félix Houphouët-Boigny (1905-1993), politician and physician; president from 1960 to 1993; from 1925 to 1940 he served as a physician; elected to the French National Assembly in 1945 and served as Ivory Coast's representative in the French government from 1946 to 1959; in his old age he was respectfully called *Le Vieux*, "The Old Man"

Koffi Konakou, a contemporary Baoulé carver; carves modern items such as baseball caps, shoes, and computers

Henri Konan Bédié (1934–), leader of the National Assembly; succeeded as president in 1993, elected president in 1995

André Latrille, French governor of Ivory Coast; he approved founding of the *Syndicat Agricole Africain* (African Agricultural Union)

Christian Lattier, contemporary sculptor famous for work made from iron covered with rope

Gnabe Opadjelé, a Bété leader; wanted to run for president in 1970 but was denied and captured by the government troops

Alassane Ouattara (1943–), economist who had worked with the International Monetary Fund before he was appointed to work out an economic recovery plan for the country in 1990; appointed prime minister in 1990

Ouattara, a contemporary Senufo artist

Gerard Santoni, a contemporary Baoulé artist

Samory Touré (–1900), a Malinké leader from Guinea; built a huge Muslim empire between 1879 and 1898; captured by the French, he was sent to Gabon where he died in exile

Marcel Treich-Laplène (1860–1890), French explorer; explored (1883) north from Assini to Kong and made treaties with local chiefs to obtain land for French

Arthur Verdier, Frenchman who administered French posts between 1858 and the late 1870s; planted Ivory Coast's first cocoa and coffee plantations

Compiled by Chandrika Kaul, Ph.D.

INDEX

Page numbers that appear in boldface type indicate illustrations

Abengourou 25, 28, 72
Abidjan 10, 12, 39, 40, 41, 45, 46, **47**, 61, 63, 65, **66, 68**, 72, **75, 76**, 79, 85, **88**, 94, **98**, 99, **100, 101**, 102, **112**, 114, 115, 117, 120, 121, 122
Abidjan Orchestral Ensemble 96
Abidji people 29, 104
Abissa festival 103
Abron people 28, 111
Aby Lagoon 11, 16, 103
acacia 20, **23**
Adjame district 100, 101
African Agricultural Union 121, 123
African buffalo **13**
African Development Bank 115
African teak 18, 116
Agboville 72
Agni people 28, 29, 44, 121
agriculture 65, 67, 68, 69, 71, 117
AIDS 63
airlines 77, 117
air plants 19
airport 77, **95**, 117
Akan people **26, 79**, 80, **91**, 114
ancestors 81, 87, 114
Angoulvant, Gov, Louis-Gabriel 37
Aniaba 31, 122
animal reserves 21, 75, 116
anopheles mosquito 23
antelopes 21, 22, 116
apartheid 59
apartments **100**
artists 93-95
Asagny Canal 39
Ashanti people 28
Assini 11, 32, 33, **102**, 103, 120, 122
Association of Customary Chiefs 45
automobiles 74, 76
avodire 18, 116
Avoisso 16

balafon **96**, 119
bananas 19, 39, 50, 65, 67, 117
Banco National Park 102
Banco River **101**
Bandama River 14, 15, 25, 30, 36, 80, 106, 116, 121
banks **66**, 81

baobab 18, 20
Baoulé Kingdom 28
Baoulé people 8, 28, 36, **37**, 80, 94, 104, 114, 119
Baptists 89
barrier islands 11, 15, 16, **102**
Basilica of Our Lady of Peace **89, 105**, 119, 122
basketmaking **26**
Bath, Youssouf 93, 122
bauxite 71, 117
beaches 11, 75, 103, **107, 108**
Belgium 35, 62, 75, 79, 114
Benin 36, 58, 121
Berlin Conference 33
Bété people 29, 36, 84-85, 114, 119
Bia River 16, 121
Biafrans 59
Binger, Louis-Gustave 33, 35, 36, 122
Bingerville 35, 94, 103, 120
Bingerville School of Art 104
birds 22, 23, 116
black-and-white colobus monkeys **22**
blackfly 63
blacksmiths **73**, 110, 111
blue marlin 108
Bobo-Dioulasso 40
Bondoukou 28, 36, 43, 111
Bouaflé 72
Bouaké 14, 25, 69, 72, 77, 80, **106**, 107, 115
Bouna 36, 37
Boundiali 24, 111
Brazzaville Conference 121
breadfruit **18**, 20
bride price 85, 85, 121
British traders 30
buffaloes **13**, 21, 116
bulbuls 22, 116
burial mounds 120
Burkina Faso 7, 15, 36, 40, 58, 73, 75, 77, 79, 96, 101, 114, 115, 120, 121, 122
buses 74, **77**
bush fallow 67
bush fowl 22, 116
bush taxi 76

Bush, George 59
bushbucks 21, 116
butterflies 106
Buyo 14

calendar 115
Canada 62
canoes 75
capital 13, 35, 36, 40, 99, 103, 104, 114, 120, 122
cargo ships **75**
cash crops 18, 39, 40, 67, 81, 82, 86, 116, 117
casino 100
cassava 30, 67, 69, 86, 117, 119
Catholic missions 31, 120, 122
Catholic schools 62, 118
Catholics 89, 106
cattle 13, 69, **85**
Cavally (town) 33
Cavally River 14, 116
Central Library 121
ceremonial stools 81, 94
ceremonies 82, 94, 119
CFA franc 115, 122
chemicals 73, 117
chevrotains 21
chief of government 114
chief of state 114
chiefs 32, 33, 38, 48, 57
chimpanzees 21, **22**, 116
Chirac, Jacques **53**
Christians 40, 85, 87, 114, 120
cities 10, 51, 62, 79, 99-111
City Theater, Cocody 102
civil rights 57
civil servants 40
climate 16-17, 23, 116
cloth, see textiles
Club Méditerranée Resort **102**, 103
coastal region 11, 16, 17, 29, 115
cobalt 71, 117
cobras 23, 116
cocoa 19, 32, 39, 41, **49**, 50, 51, 65, 67, 72, 74, 81, 103, 117, 123
Cocody district 99, 100, 102
coconut 19, 67, 72, 103, 116, 117
coffee 19, 32, 39, 50, 51, 65, 67, **68**, 72,

74, 81, 86, 103, 117, 123
colobus monkeys **22**
colonial economy 38-40
commercial crops, see cash crops
Communauté Financière Africaine
 franc 115
communication 75, 117
Constituent Assembly 43, 121
constitution 47, 52, 54, 57, 121
copper 71, 117
corvée 38, 39, 40, 42, 43
cotton 13, 41, 65, 66, 67, **69,** 85, 115,
 117
Council of Entente 47, 58115, 121
Council of Ministers 55, 114
courts 56, 114
crabs 70, 117
crocodiles 116
crop rotation 69
cultural groups 79, 114; see also
 ethnic groups
currency 115

da Costa, Soerio 29, 120, 122
Dabakala 37
dabas 67, 111
Dadié, Bernard Binlin 92, 122
Daloa 72, 84, 85, 115
dams 14, 15, 16, 65, 121
Dan people 29, 38, 86-**87, 109,** 119
Danané 59, 72, 86
dance 95, 96, 102
de Gaulle, General Charles 42, **43,**
 45, **47**
death rate 62
deforestation 116
demonstrations 51, 122
dengue fever 23
deputies 55
diamonds 71, 117
Dida people 36, 38
Dimbokro 25
Dipri festival 104
diseases 23, 31, 63
districts 38
diviners 88, 94
Divo 25, 72
drainage 15
dress 5, 91, 119
drought 51, 66, 69
drums 84, 94
dry season 116, 116
ducks 22, 116

Duncan, Daniel Kablan 122
diphtheria 63
Dupré, Pierre 92, 122
Dutch traders 30
Dyula language 91
Dyula people 27, 29, **82,** 85, 110, 114

East Africa 35
Ébrié Lagoon 11, 16, **98,** 99, 103
Ébrié people 29
École Ponty 44
Economic and Social Council 55,
 114
Economic Community of West
 African States (ECOWAS) 58, 115
economic reform 52
education 54, 60-62, 65, 118
egrets 22, 116
Egypt 35
Eisenhower, Dwight 59
elections 43, 47, 50, 52, **56,** 121, 122
electricity 15, 51, 71, 117
elephants **6,** 7, 22, 29, 88, 96, 116
empires 26-29, 120
England 35
English language 92
Ethiopia 35
ethnic groups 8, 26, 27, 43, 48, 75,
 78-87, 101, 114
Europe 29, 31, 35, 41, 73, 74
executive branch 54-55
explorers 7, 8, 29
exports 20, 46, 49, 66, 67, 74
Exxon 71

Fakaha 110, **111**
farming 12, 67, 82, 85, 117, 119; see
 also agriculture
Federation of French West Africa
 120
Ferkéssédougou 14, 16, 25, 81, 111
festivals 95, 96, 97, 103, 106
fish 22-23, 90
fishing **4, 9,** 69-**70,** 117, 119
flutes **97**
food 90-91
food crops 66, 67, 117
food products 117
foreign policy 58-60
foreigners 79, 101, 114
forestry 70-71
forests 18, 116; see also rain forests
forts 32

foutou 90, **91,** 119
France 33, 35, 40, 42, 43, 58, 60, 62,
 74, 114, 120
freedom from racial discrimination
 57
freedom of assembly 57
freedom of religion 57, 114
freedom of speech 48, 57
freedom of the press 48, 57
French citizenship 38, 44
French colony 35-47, 120
French Community 47, 48, 49, 121
French language 8, 40, **41,** 60, 92
French population 79
French settlement 31-33, 42, 43, 102,
 120
French subjects 38
French Sudan 36
French Union 44
French West Africa 35, 43, 45, 46,
 120
Front Populaire Invoirien (FPI) 123
Fulani herders 69, 83
funerals 73, 94, 106

Gabon 37, 123
Gagnoa 72, 84, 85, 115
gazelles 22, 116
Gbagbo, Laurent 52, 123
Gbon Coulibaly Museum 110, 119
Germany 35, 42, 75
Ghana 7, 11, 12, 14, 16, 26, 27, 30, 33,
 43, 58, 79, 80, 111, 114, 115, 120
goats **68,** 69
gold 26, 27, 29, 71, 117
Gomon 104
Gonfreville Mills 107
Gouéssésso **109**
Gouro people 36
Governor's Mansion, Bingerville
 104
Governor's Palace, Grand-Bassam
 103
granaries **78,** 111, 119
Grand Council 45
Grand Mosque **90**
Grand Route 76
Grand-Bassam 11, 16, 32, 35, 39, 65,
 103, 120
Grand-Lahou 11, 30, 33, 39, 104
grasses 13
grasslands, see savanna
green mambas 23, 116

Gregorian calendar 115, 118
griots 92, 119
gris-gris 102
groundnuts 83
Guere people 29
Guinea 7, 13, 21, 36, 37, 58, 79, 114, 115, 123
Guinea Highlands 11, 14, 115
Gulf of Guinea 7, 11, 12, 14, 23, 29, 30, 32, 35, 69, 71, 115, 116, 117

hang-gliding festival 97
harbors 29
hardwood trees 18, **20, 42, 70**
harmattan wind 17, 97 116
Harmattan Winds Festival 97, 119
Harris, William Wade 89, 120, 123
Harrism 89, 114, 120, 123
head tax 38
health 54, 57, 62-63, 65, 118
herons 22, **23,** 116
High Court of Justice 56
higher education 40, 60, 118
hippopotamus **21,** 116
holidays 118
hookworm 63
hornbills 22, 23, 116
hospitals 63, 118
hotels **74, 93,** 100, **106**
Houphouët-Boigny, Félix 8, **34,** 43, 44-**50,** 51, 52, 58, 89, 104, 105, 121, 122, 123
housing 73, **80,** 96, 111, 119
humidity 17
hydroelectric power 14, 15, 16, 116, 121

Id al-Adha 118
Id al-Fitr 118
imports 73, 118
Indénié Kingdom 28, 97
Independence Day 97
indigénat 38
industries 66, 73, 117
infant mortality 118
initiation 82, **86,** 94, 119
insects 23, 116
International Cocoa Organization 115
International Monetary Fund (IMF) 51, 66, 123
international relations 58

international trade 73-74
Iringo River 16
iroko 18, 116
iron 29, 71, 117
Islam 27, 28, 37 62, 89, 114, 118, 120
Israel 59, 121
Italy 35, 75
Ivoirization 49
Ivorian Popular Front Party 52, 123
ivory 22, 29, 30, 109
Ivory Coast-Burkina Faso railroad 111

Japan 74
judicial branch 56, 114
juju doctors 102

Kani 111
Katiola 27, 81, **106**
kingdoms 26
kob antelope 22, 116
Kocoumbo, A Black Student 92, 123
kola nuts 27, 29, 86
Komóe National Park 14, 21, **110,** 116, 122
Komóe River 14, 15, 28, 36, 80, 116
Konakou, Koffi 94, 123
Konan Bédié, Henri 8, 52, 53, 122, 123
Kong 27, **28,** 37, 111, 122
Kongo River 16
Koran 27
Korhogo 13, 25, 81, 110
Kossou Lake 16, 106, 116
Krinjabo 29
Kru people 26, 29, 79, 84, 108, 114

lagoons 7, 9, 11-12, 23, 25, 29, 70, 115
Lake Taabo 116
lakes 14-16, 70
languages 91-92, 114
Latrille, André 43, 123
Lattier, Christian 94, 123
Lebanon 114
legislative branch 55
Leraba River 16
Liberia 7, 12, 13, 14, 21, 29, 35, 58, 115, 122
life expectancy 62, 118
lions **10,** 21, 22, 116
literacy 60, 118
Literary Prize for Black African Expression in French 92, 123

livestock **68,** 69
Lobi people 22
Lobo River 14
lumberjacks 86

mahogany 18, 20, **33,** 70, 116
maize 30, 67, 67, **78,** 83, 91, 117, 119
malaria 23, 63
Mali 7, 26, 27, 36, 58, 74, 75, 79, 106, 114, 115, 120, 122
Malinké people 85, 92, 114, 119
mammals 10, **21**
Man (city) 13, 36, 37, 72, 86, 108-109
Mandé people 26, 27, 79, 85, 86, 114
mangabey monkeys 106
manganese 71, 117
manufacturing 65, 72-73, 117
maquis 102
marabou stork **6**
Marahoué National Park 106
Marcory district 100
markets **68, 100,** 107, 109, 110
mask dancers **95**
masks 84, **87,** 93, 94, **109**
Mauritania 36
Methodists 89
metric system 115
milk 74
millet 22, 67, 83, 85, 91, 117, 119
mining 71, 117
missionaries 31, 40
mona monkeys 106
money 115
Mongoro people **106**
monkeys **22,** 106
mosques **28,** 37, **90,** 106, 110
mosquitoes 23, 63, 116
Mount Dent 108
Mount Kahoué 109
Mount Nimba 13, 21, 109, 116
Mount Tonkou 14, 15, 109
mountains 11, 16, 108, 109
mud bricks 73, 82
Muhammad 27, 89, 120
mullet 23, 117
Municipal Council of Abidjan 48
municipalities 57, 114
museums 102, 110, 119
music 95, 102, 119
musical instruments 95, **96, 97,** 119
Muslims 27, 37, 62, 85, 87, 89, 110, 111, 123

name 8, 114, 122
National Assembly (France) 45, 123
National Assembly (Ivory Coast) 49, 52, 55, 56, 58, 114
national dish 119
National Emblem 114
National Flag 114
National Library 121
National Museum 102, 119
national parks 14, 19, 20, 106, 107
National University of Ivory Coast 61, 102
natural gas 71, 117, 122
natural resources 73
Netherlands 74
newspapers 77, 117
N'Goron Dance **24,** 96, 111
niangon 18, 116
Niger 36, 58, 121
Nigeria 30, 73, 75
Nimba Mountains 11, 13, 14
Nonaligned Movement 115
Nôtre Dame de la Paix 122
Nzi River 15
N'Zima people 103
Nzo River 14

Odienné 13, 14, 27, 37, 85, **109**
oil 65, 73, 74, 117, 122
oil fields 71, 117
oil palm **18,** 19, **64,** 66, 67, 116, 117
onchocerciasis 63
one-party rule 48, 122
Opadjelé, Gnabé 84, 123
opposition newspaper 51
Organization of African Unity (OAU) 58, 115
Ouattara (artist) 93, 123
Ouattara, Alassane 52, 53, 123

pagne 72, **78, 91, 105,** 119
palaver 48
palm oil, see oil palms
Panther Dance 110
Parti Démocratique de la Côte d'Ivoire (PDCI) 44, 47, 48, 52, 121
partridges 22, 116
petroleum 71, 118, 122
Phillips Petroleum 71
pineapple 39, 65, 67, 72, 117
pipeline **71**
plantains 67, 90, 117, 119

plantations 12, 38, 39, 40, 67, 81, 117
planters 40, 43, 49, 81
plateau 7, 11
Plateau district 99, 100
plovers 22, 116
political parties 44, 48, 51, 57, 58
polygamy 121
Pope John Paul II 89, 105, 122
population 79, 115
poro 82, 84, 119
ports 12, 13, 14, 65, **75,** 108
Portugal 35
Portuguese 7, 29, 30
pots 84, **106**
praise singers 119
prefects 56, 57
prefectures 56, 114
president 47, 55, 56, 114, 123
Presidential Palace 104
primary schools 60, 61, 118
primates 22
prime minister 47, 53, 114, 123
pygmy hippopotamuses 21, 116
pythons 23, 116

quail 22, 116
Qur'an 27
Qur'anic schools 62, 118

radios 77, 96, 117
railroad 39, 107
rain forest 7, 11, **12**-13, 16, **17,** 18, 20, 70, **107,** 115, 116
rain-forest people 29, 37
rainfall 116
rainy season 16, 116, 117
Ramadan 89
Rassemblement Démocratique Africain (RDA) 45, 121
Red Bandama River 15
red-billed hornbill **23**
reef heron **23**
reforms 43, 46, 51, 120, 121
religion 27, 87-90, 114
République de Côte d'Ivoire 8
resistance 37, 38, 84
resorts **74, 102**
rhinoceros viper **20**
rice 41, 67, **68,** 69, 83, 86, 90, 111, 117, 119
right to vote 46, 57, 121
rivers 14-16, 70

roads 18, 40, 76, **77, 110,** 116
Roman Catholic Church 88, 114
rubber 18, 19, 39, 41, 65, 67, 86, 117
Sahara desert 26, 27, 116
Sakasso 28
salt 26, 27, 29
samba 18, 70
San Pédro 13, 72, 75, 107, 117, 121
sandbars 11, 14, 29
Santoni, Gerard 94, 123
Sanwi Kingdom 28
sardines 23, 69, 72, 117
Sassandra 14, 29, 32, **108,** 120
Sassandra River 12, 14, 116
sau 20, 70, 116
Saudi Arabia 27, 89, 120
savanna 7, 11, 13-14, 16, 20, **23,** 26, 66, 69, 110, 115
schools 40
sculpture **83, 93,** 94, 118
seaport **75,** 117
seasons 16-17, 116
secondary education 60, 61, 118
Senegal 36, 40
Senufo people **24,** 27, 28, 37, **73, 78,** 81, **82,** 83, 84, 93, 94, 96, 110, 111, 114, 118, 119
sheabutter 20
shells **24,** 25
shifting agriculture 67
ships **75**
shrimp 70, 72, 117
sipo 18, 116
slaves 26, 30, **31**
sleeping sickness 23
snakes **20,** 23
soccer 119
social security 119
Socialist Party 42
softwood 18
Songhai 26, 27, 120
sorcery 88
sorghum 67, 85, 117
Soubré 14, 84
South Africa 35, 59, 122
Soviet Union 121
Spain 79
sports arena **101**
St. Paul's Cathedral **88,** 100
State Security Court 56
stilt dance 109
storytellers 92

subprefects 56, 57
sugarcane 65, 67, 111, 117
Supreme Court 56
Switzerland 79
Syndicat Agricole Africain (SAA) 43, 121, 123

Taabo Lake 16
Tabou 108
Tadio Lagoon 11, 15, 104
Tai National Park 19, 21, **107,** 116
Taylor, Charles 58, **59**
telephones **46,** 77, 117
televisions 77, 107, 117
temperature 16, 116
termites **23,** 116
terns 22, 116
Territorial Assembly 44, 45, 47
textiles 72, 91, 107, 110, 117
thatch roofs 73, 82, 119
Tiagba 104
timber 18, 39, 65, 66, 70, 107
Togo 58
Touba 25, 109
Toumodi 25
Touré, Samory 37, 120, 123
tourism 59, 73-74, 75, 107, 108
trade 32, 46, 47, 73-74, 75, 118
trade routes 26, 27, 120
transportation 75-77, 117
treaties 32, 33, 36, 123
tree hyraxes 21, 116

trees 17, **18,** 20, 94, 116
Treich-Laplène, Marcel 33, 123
Treichville Cultural Center 102
Treichville district **100,** 101, 102
tribal chief **32;** see also chiefs
tsetse flies 23, 69, 116
tuberculosis 63
tuna 23, 69, 72, 117

United Nations Children's Fund (UNICEF) 63
United Nations Educational, Scientific, and Cultural Organization (UNESCO) 19
United States 59, 60, 62, 75, 79, 114
University of Abidjan 121
University of Côte d'Ivoire 61, 118
Upper Volta, see Burkina Faso

vaccination 63
Vatican 105
vegetables 67
vendors 102
Verdier, Arthur 32, 123
vice-president 122
Vichy government 42, 43
village chiefs 38, 57, 94; see also chiefs
villages 80, 99, 101-111
Voltaic people 26, 79, 81, 114
Vridi 71, 73, 117
Vridi Canal 46, 117, 120, 121

Waraniene 110
warthog **21**
washermen **101**
waterbuck **21,** 22
weapons 25
weavers **82,** 110
West Africa 7, 26, 35, 37, 47, 50, 75, 91, 112
West African Economic Community 115
White Bandama River 15, 28
wildlife 20, 110, 116
wind 17, 116
wood carvers **37,** 84, **93,** 94
wood products 117
World Bank 51, 66
World Health Organization (WHO) 63
World Wars 41, 42
writers 92

xylophone 96
Yago, Cardinal Bernard 51
Yamoussoukro 13, 15, 44, 58, 61, **74,** 76, 77, 80, **89, 90, 95,** 99, 104-106, 115, 119, 122
yams 22, 67, **69,** 90, 117, 119
yaws 63
yellow fever 23, 36, 63, 120
Zala 97
Zouan-Hounien 59

About the Author

Patricia K. Kummer writes and edits textbook materials and nonfiction books for children and young adults. She earned a Bachelor of Arts degree in history from the College of St. Catherine in St. Paul, Minnesota, and a Master of Arts degree in history from Marquette University. Before starting her career in publishing, Ms. Kummer taught social studies at the junior-high/middle-school level.

Since then, she has written about American, African, and Asian history for textbook publishers and "A Guide to Writing and Speaking," in World Book's *Word Power Library*, as well as editing many books in the America the Beautiful and the From Sea to Shining Sea series for Children's Press. Ms. Kummer is a member of Chicago Book Clinic, Chicago Women in Publishing, and Children's Reading Round Table.

Ms. Kummer lives in Lisle, Illinois, with her husband, Walter, and their three children, Kevin, Kathleen, and Kristopher.